To Malcol.

With Bes

The Author

CW01429348

Richard Tompkinson

Ecclisgray. 1999.

Deer-stalking in the
Scottish Highlands 1940–1990

Deer-stalking

in the Scottish Highlands
1940–1990

MICHAEL FORSYTH-GRANT

The Pentland Press
Edinburgh – Cambridge – Durham – USA

First published in 1999 by
The Pentland Press Ltd
1 Hutton Close,
South Church
Bishop Auckland
Durham

ISBN 1-85821-647-8

DEER-STALKING
Typeset in Goudy 13/15
by Carnegie Publishing, Chatsworth Road, Lancaster
Printed and bound by Bookcraft Ltd, Bath

To Kai (Dr Karl Hans Miedler of Austria) and my elder son Maurice, who have shared so many experiences with me

Contents

Illustrations

Preface

It is nearly sixty years since G.K. Whitehead produced that bible for all deer stalkers, *The Deer Stalking Grounds of Great Britain and Ireland*. The cost of this Deer Encyclopedia was then six Guineas. Today, such a book could not be purchased for £250!

I have used Whitehead's book to great advantage in renting or stalking some 55 forests that are amongst those mentioned therein. It is an absolute mine of useful information.

I would not have the tenacity to try to compete with G.K. Whitehead, whose knowledge of Red Deer has been unrivalled by any other for half a century, but in *Stalking Grounds* little mention is made of personalities, the costs of renting fifty years ago and now at the present time, and anecdotes of how some of the stalkers and landowners have fared in a much-changing scene.

The fifty-year era between 1940 and 1990 will

never be repeated, and before all is forgotten, it may be useful to have some record of the happenings in those years in the Scottish Highlands. That is why I have written this book and I hope the reader will glean some information on the past, and hopefully have a laugh at some of the anecdotes that I have told.

Chapter One

1940–55

The last detailed and authoritative book on Red Deer stalking grounds by G. Kenneth Whitehead was published nearly sixty years ago, since when there have been so many changes. I have been lucky enough to have stalked 55 different deer forests between 1940 and 1996, and it may be of historical interest to record the changing season, not only of deer ground, but of the deer themselves, the changing scene, the stalking personalities and the financial aspect of the whole scenario.

In 1940 as a nineteen-year-old midshipman I was appointed to serve in a warship in Loch Ewe, to which I travelled from Scapa Flow. I had never been further north nor west than Aberdeenshire, and the journey through Wester Ross was a real eye-opener. Although I had shot for ten years with rifle and shotgun, including a very few Roe Deer as quarry, I had absolutely no experience of Red Deer.

I was very lucky when the police constable at Gairloch introduced me to the Head Stalker of Flowerdale Forest, old McNicol, who invited me to try some Red Deer stalking. I fairly jumped at the chance. Flowerdale was most picturesque, with wonderful views over Loch Maree and to Skye. I had some wonderful days out with McNicol but I failed to score! I missed quite an easy stag with his 6.5 mm Mannlicher, probably because I had not fired a trial shot at a target. After a spell in Channel destroyers, I was posted to Fort William as a Trainee Commanding Officer of Coastal Force Units. I was 20.

I had a wonderful spell of three weeks in August 1941 at Fort William. My parents were friendly with the late Lochiel, and he very kindly gave me permission to shoot on Tor Castle. Many a grouse and a few wild fowl I shot between Fort William and Corpach – all open moor in those days, always accompanied by Robertson, the keeper.

Robertson told me they had a small area of hill ground marching with Achnacarry, and we could try that one evening. All our ground was bare, but there was a nice stag twenty yards over the march, which Robertson said we could not shoot. After spying this stag for twenty minutes, laced with liberal drams of whisky, Robertson allowed me to have a go. The stag dropped stone dead to my shot and we dragged it to our side of the march

The Author (left) with Ewan Orminston, the largest Venison dealer in UK 1939–54 (the Author is 6 feet, Ewan is considerably taller)

before it was gralloched. I had no qualms about this, as the neighbouring ground was let to Ewan Ormiston, the biggest venison-dealer in Scotland for many years and later a good friend of mine. In any case, quite a few of his stags were killed by Army personnel, even with machine guns. Anyway, I was delighted. This was my first stag ever.

I gained some superb sport with Robertson, though thereafter we restricted ourselves to our own ground, and one day, within fifty yards of four stags, I missed. My fingers were so cold that I could not move the bolt of the Mannlicher, and we had a blank day. I had a feverish cold at the time and when I returned to our Base at Fort William's Grand Hotel, I wallowed in whisky until I was pretty inebriated. A fellow officer, equally tipsy, threw a dart through a window, breaking the glass, and I went to congratulate him on his appalling piece of vandalism. This was Philip Wayre, the distinguished TV broadcaster on wild life, author, owner of the Norfolk Wild Life Park and the Otter Sanctuary at Bungay. We became life-long friends.

By the time I left Fort William, I was completely hooked on Red Deer stalking, but my naval duties prevented me from stalking again for seven years. I had excellent sport shooting birds in Kent in 1942–43 while serving in Motor Gunboats at Ramsgate, shooting wolves in North Russia in late

1944/45, and shooting elephant and hippo in Sierra Leone in 1946. In 1947, back home at last, I telephoned my friends in Gairloch for information about, and prospects of, Red Deer in Wester Ross. They told me to come over and stay in the Gairloch Hotel, and said that they would arrange something. The 'something' they arranged was not to my taste. It was pure poaching, and I declined the offers, mostly made by the hall porter at the hotel and various local shepherds! I did accept the offer of the hotel 'boots' to take a drive up Glen Docherty at night to see what others did. Every fish lorry seemed to carry an ex-Army .303 rifle, and they slaughtered the deer on the roadside by the headlights. I was really pretty shocked by what I saw and heard. The police and gamekeepers seemed powerless to stop it. It nearly put me off shooting Red Deer altogether, and I returned home absolutely empty-handed.

In 1948 I was invited by Sir James Caird, Bart., to try for a stag on his grouse moor, Glen Farquhar and Delavaird in Kincardineshire. Sir James was a self-made shipping tycoon/millionaire, who had transformed these moors, often obtaining 200 brace of grouse or more in a day. It was ideal ground-driving territory, about 10,000 acres, at the head of the River Bervie, with Glen Dye and Glenbervie adjacent. The occasional Red Deer came off Glen Dye.

Farquharson was the Head Keeper, and although around 65, was energetic and resourceful. I shot a stag where the River Bervie, at its source, can be crossed without even jumping.

On the death of Sir James, who financed the Painted Hall at R.N. College, Greenwich, Glen Farquhar was broken up and sold. It is now all covered in dense Sitka Spruce. The River Bervie is totally sterile at its source through acid rain, and the once magnificent Glen Farquhar Lodge is a home for very handicapped people.

There is no game to be seen, only Hoody Crows and hawks (1990). Then in 1950 I read in the *Sporting Press* that Captain and Mrs Hunt had taken over the Invergarry Hotel, between Fort Augustus and Fort William, and were advertising Red Deer safaris. This I decided to sample, and booked in for part of the stag season, 1951. I was not to be disappointed.

On my way to Invergarry, I spent two nights and a day at Dalmunzie Hotel, Glenshee. The owner, Dennis Winton, also owned Dalmunzie Deer Forest, and I rented a day on this.

The hotel had originally been the home of the Birkmyre family – millionaires of South Africa – who had built a light railway up the glen with a zigzag route and points to change. This took about 1,000 feet off the climb up the glen. The young stalker, Kennedy, drove the train, and I discovered his uncle was Head Stalker at Glenfeshie, considered the best deer forest in Scotland. Using a standard U.S. Winchester Springfield 30 cal. Sniper's Rifle with telescopic sight, I shot my first stag that day at around noon. We dragged this to the railtrack and stalked on. While on the march with Rhidorroch Deer Forest (Invercauld Estate), we spied a large herd of stags with a few hinds coming over the march. Kennedy told me to take my pick – one beast only. There were nearly 100 stags in that herd. On and on came the beasts, obviously disturbed from the adjacent forest. I picked what I thought was the best-bodied stag, and it fell dead to the shot. We dragged this to the rail head, and were 200 yards above it when I spied a single travelling stag approaching in the failing light, about 150 yards distant. We dropped to the ground, and I shot this stag at around 100 yards. We had only a short distance to go to get both stags on the train's flat wagon.

Next day I set off for Invergarry Hotel and introduced myself to Captain Leslie and Mrs Bunty Hunt. They were leasing three deer forests, Garrygualach, Glengarry and Killiechonate.

For the next fortnight, I stalked Garrygualach and Invergarry, the former with Jock MacAskill and the second with Stewart, both very competent, and I averaged one beast per day. I paid £5 for every stag shot, and the carcase belonged to the hotel. MacAskill was an ex-Commando, aged about 34 at the time. He was also an expert salmon ghillie. Stewart was much the same age – a professional trapper.

On one occasion I gave my rifle to my cousin, Malcolm Forsyth-Grant, a Lieutenant, RN, so that he could shoot his first stag, which he did one late afternoon opposite the Tomdoon Hotel. Loch Garry was quite small then – before being dammed for hydro-electricity – the Garry flowed in front of the hotel down the glen to Loch Oich at the bottom. Next day a youth from Greenfield Lodge (owned by Miss Ellice), drove a small grey petrol/paraffin tractor with a transport box to collect the stag. In turning, he got hopelessly bogged in a beat drain, and two of us were unable to free it. We therefore forded the River Garry up to our navels, and freezing cold, asked 'mine host', Hector Grant – a Highland Games Heavy Athlete – for help. First we drained a bottle of rum to keep the cold out! Hector and two colleagues escorted us to a boat on Loch Garry and this time we boated over. The tractor was soon de-bogged with levers and planks, and we set off on the three miles to Greenfield Farm, with tractor and stag. It was exhausting work, so next day I decided we would have a quiet rest day at Fort William with my cousin, his wife and two lady guests of mine at the hotel. I had just ordered sandwiches in the lounge of the Grand

Hotel, when Kitty Renny Tailyour said we were all going to walk up Ben Nevis! Not only did we do this, but went to a Highland Dance in Invergarry Hall that evening, and we stalked the next day. It is worth noting that Jock MacAskill, with Mrs Hunt as his 'rifle', had the same experience later that season, but he had no rum and was off sick with 'flu for the rest of the season!

Garrygualach was a nice forest, and not very steep, although it marched with Glenkingie, and across the road to Garry with Loch Quoich (Charles William's M.P.).

Glengarry was different. Much of it was very steep and picturesque, Ben Tee in the middle being of great historic interest. It was rented from the Forestry Commission, and Garrygualach from Miss Ellice. The food at Invergarry Hotel was excellent, mostly cooked by Mrs Hunt, and the bedrooms, sparsely furnished, were adequate. Arrangements for drying clothes were good, though public room furniture was rubbish. But what did real stalkers want? The costs of stalking were low. I paid £5 per stag shot, and the hotel kept the carcase.

In 1952, I rented Achncarry North from an agent, probably Captain Percy Wallace. It belonged to Lochiel. Rent was £120 per week for 10 stags, a five-day week with stalker, ghillie and ponyman provided, estate to keep the deer. My base was Invergarry Hotel. I found Achnacarry North rather boring – not interesting scenically except for the opportunity to gaze on historic Loch Arkaig ('Flight of the Heron' and all that!). The vast rounded hills were bald except for white grass. Clunes Hill to the south looked much more attractive.

Stevenson was the Head Stalker, and doubled as old Lochiel's piper. He was a dour fellow with little to impart, and only average skill as a stalker. He could be very bad-tempered, and once when the ponyman botched our stag by showing himself, Stevenson seized my rifle and emptied the magazine with shots round the scared fellow!

There was to be no stalking at North Achnacarry on Saturdays, and being very fit then – I was 31 – I rented the day from Leslie Hunt and went out with Stewart on Glengarry. The forest was pretty empty that day, but as we approached the Achnacarry march, we saw a stag grazing towards us.

Stewart would not let me shoot it on the Achnacarry ground, although it was mine by lease, but I shot it as it crossed the march fence, which its dead corpse straddled.

My second week at Achnacarry was terribly wet and, it being evening, I drove back for nearly an hour to Invergarry with the heater on the warm-up.

On arrival home that autumn, I contracted 'flu, which persisted nearly all that winter.

In the summer of 1953 my father died, and I had too much on my hands for deer-stalking, except for one day at Hunthill in Angus, where, with Stalker Chrystal, I shot four stags with four shots – separate stalks with my Mannlicher schonaeur .375 with open sights! This was the best I ever achieved in over 50 years of stalking! Hunthill in 1953 was classed as a top grouse moor, and deer were very secondary. It was not extra steep, as befits a good grouse-driving moor, and scenically it was very pleasant. It was then about 25,000 acres, owned by Dalhousie Estates. Chrystal was a good competent stalker.

In 1945 I started off by sub-renting Gaick from Ewan Ormiston, originally a butcher at Newtonmore, who became the biggest buyer of venison in Scotland between 1940–53, and tenanted large numbers of deer forests. The owner of Gaick in 1954 was Sir Ewan Macpherson Grant, Bart., of Ballindalloch, who had recently inherited Gaick, Glenfeshie, Invereshie and Glentromie, besides the vast lands of Ballindalloch and Craigo. He was a very close friend of mine and as a boy was brought up on the neighbouring estate of Craigo, Montrose. He inherited these properties and title around 1952 but he was not at all interested in Red Deer stalking, and sold off all the deer forests and grouse moors around Kincraig about 1960. But I digress. Gaick is part of the Cairn Gorm massif and one of the steepest forests in Scotland, but in 1954 it had the most excellent zigzag footpaths, so that climbing to over 3,000 feet was not all that exhausting. The forest extends to about 30,000 acres.

The Head Stalker (1954) was Sutherland, and the Second Stalker was Cameron Ormiston (Ewan's son). Both were pretty competent. I shot some stags there, but two incidents in particular stand in my memory. Sutherland and I were on a ridge at about 3,000 feet, looking into a steep valley, and a strong breeze was blowing along the ridge. There were several large herds of deer 1,500 feet below us. Any experienced stalker knows the vagaries of cross-currents and downdraughts in these Scottish Mountains. Suddenly, to my horror, the deer below caught our wind and cleared the glen. Our struggle to get to the ridge, ascending some 2,000 feet, had been totally in vain. We had to descend and climb another high ridge before we were able to see more deer in a different glen.

The track from the stalker's house to a tarmac road seemed about 10 miles long, and very unsuitable for an ordinary car, which is all I had. Motoring down the road, I spied a nice herd several hundred yards off the track across the small river which flowed down the glen. I waded this –

it was very cold! – and round a knoll I came face to face with a fine stag, at a range of under 20 yards. We both stared at each other. Slowly I got the rifle to my shoulder and found the image in the scope so large that I could not identify the heart. I would have given a fortune for open sights. While I was trying to find a good aiming spot, the stag bolted, and I never got a shot.

During the Spring of 1954 I had read in the gossip columns in the *Sunday Express* that a premier stalking hotel had been opened in the wilds of Scotland – namely Ben More Lodge, off the Lairg to Lochinver road, so I sent for details and arranged to stay there for a fortnight after leaving Gaick. The terms sounded reasonable: £32 per week for bed, breakfast, pack lunch and dinner with stalking included, hotel to keep the carcase. Alternatively, if one paid £37 per week, half the stags shot became one's own property, or one could sell them back to the hotel. I opted for the latter arrangement.

The Lodge, of all-timber construction, was situated beside Loch Ailsh, where one could fish free for trout. A dirt track ran from the Lairg/Lochinver tarmac road to the Lodge alongside the River Oykel. There was no telephone, and electric light was supplied by the hotel diesel generator, which was shut down between 10 p.m. and 7 a.m. The food was good, the beds and rooms comfortable, and the Lady Manageress very pleasant and competent. There were only two other guests staying in the hotel. The first was the Chairman of Renters, who was only interested in salmon fishing on the Oykel, and the second was the High Sheriff of Hampshire. The owner, the Hon. Francis de Moleyns, was widower of Lady Ross (of Ross Rifle fame), and her vast estates included three major deer forests and two grouse moors.

Over my first breakfast, I gathered there had been an almighty row between de Moleyns and the two resident stalkers, who had both walked out! However, two low-ground keepers from the Estate grouse moors at Edderton/Kincardine had been press-ganged to take their place. I was allocated one MacIntosh, to whom the East Beat had been deputed. The High Sheriff had the more interesting ground, which included Ben More Assynt, marching with that renowned forest of Lady Rootes, Inchnadamph.

I had an excellent week with MacIntosh, and averaged one stag per day, which the two of us had to collect with a good estate pony. The High Sheriff did not fare nearly so well. He was at loggerheads with his stalker, and I think they only had two stags for their week.

That Sunday another guest turned up unexpectedly to come and stalk. It was a double booking, and the confusion had been caused by lack of communication, in other words, no telephone. The new guest turned up with his mother, who was very rich and I think a daughter of Hulton, the publisher of *Picture Post*.

There were places for only two rifles, and as I had enjoyed an excellent week, I decided I would go and stay at the Bridge Hotel, Bonar Bridge on the Sunday night, and see if I could stalk Alladale or Deanich, the other two estate forests, which were totally unlet.

So after breakfast on Monday I set off to explore Alladale Forest – a few miles distant in territory quite unknown to me. I found the Lodge, and the ponyman, who was chopping sticks for the fire. He told me the Head Stalker had already left to stalk on his own, but I said I had paid for the stalking, and he must take me out on the forest and hopefully find the Stalker. This we did by lighting a smoke fire, and by 10.30 a.m., I was in company with the Head Stalker, Donald Clark. There was also a Second Stalker, McLeod.

In the late afternoon, we spied a large herd of deer, about 250 strong, grazing a steep hillside. We were on the ridge and the deer, stags and hinds, were grazing into the wind below us. Leading near the front was a very large stag that was very prominent, and Donald told me to take this when I could. I was below the ridge skyline lying on a very steep slope, and after a few moments, the blood was rushing to my head.

Something at the rear of the herd disturbed them and they came forward at a trot, disturbing the beast I was hoping to get. Donald said it was now or never, and I fired. The range was about 150 yards, and I was firing steeply downhill. Recovering from the smoke of the discharge and the concussion, I could see that my stag was on its back, legs in the air, moving quite vigorously, but it was obvious that the wound was mortal and the beast was dying. The large herd rushed forward, leaving the big stag now still where it fell. It was a magnificent 14 pointer, and I was later told that only three of this calibre were shot in Scotland that year. I still have the antlers.

Next day I was joined by my close friend, Cmdr. Colin Keay, and I sent him out with McLeod, while I stalked with Donald Clark. That day I successfully stalked a stag uphill, watched by Donald, who judged it unsafe for two people to stalk the beast in full sight of the stag and some 14 hinds. After a very long belly-crawl, I shot the stag dead with my open sighted .375 Mannlicher. Donald thought the calibre was too large, and suggested I used my Winchester Springfield 30 cal. sniper rifle with scope sight next day. He thought highly of my skill! He also told me that one should never try to shoot a moving stag, with which I heartily agreed.

Next day Donald took me in to four stags, and told me which one to shoot. It was quite a close, easy shot. Not only did I miss the stag, but I had mistakenly fired at another. My great reputation was now in tatters and the stag went off at a trot, reappearing on the side of the valley about 250 yards distant. I glassed them through my rifle scope and Donald pointed out the one I should have targeted. I can't think what made me do it, but

Benmore, Sutherland, 1954. Stalker, Stewart on left

my finger tightened on the trigger, the glen echoed to the shot, and the trotting stag fell as dead as a shot-gunned rabbit! Donald and I just stared at one another. My reputation was restored.

Colin and I then decided to return to Ben More and shoot some further stags there. Colin, however, had to leave, and I was alone, stalking with MacIntosh.

One day, stalking two lone stags on very flat

Cairngorms 1954

ground between the Rivers Cassley and Oykel, MacIntosh got me into superb position and told me to shoot both stags if possible. They were not difficult, and I scored a right and left. We then had a long trek back to Ben More Lodge to get the pony. We loaded one stag back to the Lodge. Then we took the pony back again for the second stag. This took us several hours and when we finally arrived with the second stag, we found that the Manageress was in a terrible state and was about to organise a search party. It had been pitch dark for several hours, but all was well.

The next – and my last day – I shot a stag as we were finishing the day and the light was going. Then we spied a lone stag standing very prominently on a peat hillock. It was an easy shot and such was my reputation, that MacIntosh whispered, 'I wouldn't like to be that stag.' I missed it clean, and never saw it again. Such a demon is over-confidence.

That was the end of my stalking for 1954. I was very pleased with Ben More, and by the time I left and settled my account for Board, Lodging and Stalking, with the rebate for the stags I had shot, the cost was negligible. The High Sheriff was not so fortunate. He spent most of the day arguing with his stalker and after a fortnight had only three stags for all his hard labour.

Chapter Two

1955–59

Having had such a successful season at Ben More, I would like to have returned, but for some reason or other it was not to be. The vast estates embracing the deer forests of Ben More, Alladale and Deenich (sometimes the latter two are called Freewater), the grouse moors at Edderton and Kincardine, the salmon fishings in the Oykel and Kyle and Sutherland, and two or three hotels, together with Balnagowan Castle went on sale. It was the biggest acreage of land of the century to date in U.K. to be offered for sale. It was sold by C.W. Ingrams of Edinburgh, and the auction of 32 lots was conducted by John Ingram, a distant relative of mine. The Grill Room of the North British (renamed in 1995 as The Balmoral), Edinburgh's most prestigious hotel, was the venue. It was packed. John Ingram asked for offers of half a million. No reply. The first bid came at £300,000 for all 32 lots and within minutes the whole lot had been sold for £420,000 to one buyer. I had been asked to buy Lot 16 – net salmon fishings in the Kyle of Sutherland – but the whole lot went in one bid to the exclusion and disappointment of the many who only wanted one of the 32 lots. By 1995, Mohammed el Fayed of Harrods had bought Balnagowan Castle and within a year had spent around £3,000,000 refurbishing it alone. The value of the whole estate today would be in excess of £100,000,000.

In the Spring of 1955, the deer forest of Inverlael, near Ullapool, was advertised for sale, and I was soon in touch with the large firm of estate agents in London who were putting it on the market. It was the property of the Hon. George Rous, son of Lord Stradbroke. It comprised about 23,000 acres, rising from sea level at Loch Broom to over 3,000 feet on Ben Dearg.

After some correspondence, I was offered a deal. I could buy the estate, including houses and a rather decrepit lodge, for £13,500, plus the sheep at valuation. The sellers were most co-operative. In August 1955, I was commanding a warship in a big naval exercise at Invergordon, and having a Sunday off, took my car to visit the property, shown to me by the shepherd overseer, Mr Mac-Rae. Although I was very taken by the scenery, I asked the selling agents if I could stalk the place for the stag season of 1955. If I failed to buy it, I would pay the proper rent. If I did buy it, there would be no rent to pay.

In Sept/October, I marshalled my resources. No-one was available at Inverlael except 17-year-old Robert, son of the shepherd. I recruited Bill Whyte, a 22-year-old salmon fisher from Montrose, who had just completed his National Service fighting the bandits in Malaya, and Willie Harvey, a 17-year-old fisherman from Johnshaven. I hired three good deer-carrying ponies from Allison, a dealer in Dingwall, who also provided deer saddles. The cost of this hire, ponies and saddles, was £5 per pony per week. My Sunbeam III car was totally unfit for Highland tracks, so I hired a Land Rover – a comparative rarity in 1955 – from MacRae & Dick in Inverness. I paid Robert MacRae, Willie Whyte and Willie Harvey a weekly wage, and paid board for the two Willies in a 'Bed & Breakfast' in Ullapool. I stayed in the Royal there, as I knew the proprietress quite well. She had previously been 'mine hostess' at the Loch Maree Hotel and was well known in the West Highland hotel business.

On the first day I mustered my forces, three men, three ponies and the Land Rover, and entered the great glen below Ben Dearg.

The glen, or valley, was most impressive, for we started off at about 60 feet above sea level and looked up at the massive cliffs of Ben Dearg, which

Author (mounted) with Robert Macrae and Bill Whyte. Inverlael
1955

towered above us at over 3,000 feet. The other side of the glen was not nearly so steep, rising to around 2,000 feet and ascended by very well kept paths and cross drains. The Land Rover was of little use except for the first mile from the Lodge, and the lower slopes of Ben Dearg were heavily afforested (Forestry Commission). About the second day, we succeeded in making the ridge of which Ben Dearg was the highest bastion. For two or three miles into the glen, the Ben Dearg ridge was far too steep for stalkers or ponies, but some miles further up, the ridge was accessible to both and to reach the summit of Ben Dearg was not too difficult.

1955 had been one of the best summers in Scotland for some years, but sadly the weather that late September and October was abominable. We were plagued by snow, rain and fog. Inverleal Forest is shaped like a boot – the 'foot' extended along Loch Broom to march with Leckmeln, then curves inland to march with Rhidorroch. Above the 'ankle', Inverlael, runs north-east for 14 miles to a tin-roofed 'lodge', or rather bothy, called Glenbeg, to which there was no access, between Inverlael and Glenbeg, except by the pony track. Half a mile beyond Glenbeg was Deanich Lodge, only accessible then by a track via Alladale, again of about 14 miles. Among the assets which emerged during the negotiations over buying

Inverlael, was included a set of maps showing massive Hydro-electric tunnels through the forest, and this had obviously depressed the asking price because of the poaching that was likely to be prevalent while the tunnelling was in process.

However, to return to my own stalking operations. We had a difficult first week, but managed a few stags in spite of the bad weather. Willie Harvey was always left with the ponies far down the glen, and proved an excellent, if inexperienced ponyman. In resisting the cold in driving snow for long periods, he proved most adept, with an oversize Army greatcoat enveloping most of his torso.

Returning to the hotel one evening, I had a message left in my room inviting me to Sunday lunch at Foich Lodge, owned by Lady Irene and Capt. Claude Crawford, who were close forest neighbours beside Ben Dearg and marched with Braemore, with which Inverleal too had a common frontier of several miles.

I duly lunched with the Crawfords, who had a nice lodge, Foich, and an excellent show in their small garden of hydrangeas. After lunch, Capt. Crawford asked me to meet the Braemore stalker, a staunch Seceder (!), and had to ask him first whether he would be prepared to speak to a stranger on a Sunday! The whole exercise had been quite a success for me, but when I returned to the hotel, Mrs Mackenzie gave me a queer look and said she was glad to see me alive! Apparently some very weird happenings were attributed to the Crawfords. Claude had been in the Brigade of Guards, and was liable to recall. Lady Irene, daughter of the Marquis of Camden, was not prepared to let him go, and shot him in the foot (accidently?), with the result that he was passed unfit for war service. Next, she allegedly gave a stalker she did not like sandwiches laced with strychnine! Fortunately, the stalker was suspicious and failed to eat them! Next, one of the best stalking ponies at Foich was shot dead by someone with a grudge.

The Crawfords told me that they had been at war with poaching '——', who had fired on their Land Rover with .303 rifles. The police were involved, and Robert Churchill, the world-famous gun forensic scientist, was to examine the Land Rover. He reported that the bullets had been fired from within the cab – not from outside it. There the story stopped. Strangely, I had read all this in the *Sunday Post* before I had even met the Crawfords. Then on two separate occasions, there had been two 'suicides' in the gunroom at Foich, at least one being a Crawford relation. Further, the neighbouring 'laird' at Leckmeln, Mr McLaverty, had been in dispute with Lady Irene, and his Lodge had been burnt down, whereupon he fled to Elgin and never returned. How much was true and how much mere gossip, I do not know, but it was not surprising that Mrs Mackenzie said she was glad to see me return alive!

The next week at Inverlael was one of accidents. First Robert sprained his ankle and could stalk no more that season, but he was invaluable as a consultant. Then one of the ponies went down with saddle sore, and I had to get the vet from Gairloch – quite expensive.

One day I was reduced to Willie and one pony, and I decided to stalk alone, reaching a ridge about 2,500 feet up and asking Willie to stay in the glen bottom and try to look out for me. This was no easy task for him, as I tried to reach the ridge unseen by any of the local deer, taking advantage of every burn and gully that I could. At last I was on the ridge, and what a beautiful view I had! I could see the Western Isles up to 50 miles away, and I spent some time getting my wind back and admiring the superb vista.

What I did not realise was that low clouds driving in from the west were closing in. I was looking under them and never saw what was coming. Suddenly I could not see fifty yards for the fog. I started to descend, and this was highly dangerous. I did not know the ground and twice landed at the top of a rock-face precipice. I was very glad when I had managed to drop 1,500 feet below the fog.

We stalked away all that week, and I had some

naval guests, but the weather was awful. One day we never left the car. The wind and rain were quite horrendous.

I had enjoyed my fortnight, although it was not a stalking success. The paths were magnificent, and had Robert been fit the second week, and had the pony not been incapacitated by saddle sores, my decision might have been different. I decided not to buy the forest, for which I would have had to sell my best low-ground farm. The value of each was much the same – £14,000. I parted on the best of terms with the selling agents and the Hon. George Rous. Inverlael remained unsold for a further 2½ years and was then sold to Dr Morgan S. Whiteridge for the same price that had been asked of me.

Returning home, I was invited by one of my co-directors of Jos. Johnston Ltd to have a couple of days stalking on Glenisla. I took this up without hesitation, and set off with Douglas the stalker. Glenisla Forest is quite small – estimated under 4,000 acres. It consists of a ridge march with Glenprosen Forest, then a bit of Glendoll, thence via Tulchan back into Glenisla. Tulchan had been a renowned forest, owned by the Earl of Airlie, and at this time was being sold to the Earl of Inchcape. It had a record of erratic and alcoholic Head Stalkers. Not so old Douglas of Glenisla. He was a splendid old fellow, then about 65, and just about to retire to relations on Dartmoor! We got on extremely well, and he just pointed out the various march limits and sometimes the stags he wanted me to shoot, and left me to get on with it.

I thoroughly enjoyed my two days and shot several stags. The limit for the season was 15. On my return, John Stansfeld, who had only retired a few days previously, asked me if I would be interested in taking it next year, and I told him I would be delighted. So that was the end of the stalking season of 1955.

I duly rented Glenisla from owner Henry Gibb for October 1956, and asked various guests to stay with me in the Glenisla Hotel. Meantime, I had contacted a horse dealer in my village (St Cyrus) to train a Norwegian pony to carry deer, for which I had bought a deer saddle. The pony soon got used to the smell of blood, and by stalking time, was quite able to carry stags, so I had the pony, Bergen, stabled at Glenisla.

Glenisla being so small – under 4,000 acres – it was not advisable to stalk it six days a week, so I went back to Dalmunzie, twice the size of Glenisla, and part-rented that, so that we could stalk every day of the week. Douglas left us pretty much to our own devices at Glenisla (sometimes referred to as Glencally), and was happy to work the pony and collect the dead stags with Bergen. At Dalmunzie, McLeod, the stalker, was a much more alive character, and pretty competent. We had some good results on both forests. That winter, I felt Bergen deserved better pasture for all the good work done, and I limed the grass. This was a fatal error, and shortly afterwards Bergen died of grass sickness. I felt great remorse that I had been so stupid. Any old hat could have told me that Highland and Norwegian ponies thrive best on coarse moorland grasses, but I had never asked about this, and so an excellent pony was lost through crass stupidity.

In 1957 I approached the Factor of Glen Dye and asked about stalking there. At that time Glen Dye seemed very neglected and the owner was not interested in either grouse or deer. In the 1920s it had been a showpiece for driven grouse, and although primarily a grouse moor, it had a good population of stags.

Glen Dye Lodge and Estate is very easily reached from my home in forty minutes. The road bypasses Laurencekirk and is roughly the line where the Vale of Strathmore meets the Howe o' The Mearns, the Clatterin Brig, at the foothills of the Grampians. The road then ascends very steeply to Cairn o' Mount, and you have breasted the first main ridge of the Grampians. This is really where the Glen Dye stalking starts. Some miles downhill one is in a great valley, looking up to Mount Battoch of nearly 3,000 feet and crossing the

Water of Dye, which runs through the Forest and it is here that the Stalker's house is situated.

I met the Head Stalker for the first time, one Dan Dowall and his assistant or Second Stalker, Ferrier, I already knew the Ferrier family as the Second Stalker's father was underkeeper of the Balnamoon Estate in Angus. Dan Dowall was about 50 years of age, and although he liked a good dram, was remarkably fleet of foot.

A pony and ponyman were included, and the rate was £5 per stag, the venison to be the property of the estate. We were able to drive up the newly-made estate roads – tracks would be a better description – for about three miles, to where there were stables for the ponies. I was determined to explore Glen Dye very fully, and decided that as the ground was so extensive, there was no need to consider other areas for the 1957 and 1958 seasons. Stag rents were rising, and £5 per stag seemed pretty reasonable.

It was not an easy place to stalk, being grouse moor. There were very few steep gulleys, and it was generally very flat. None of Mount Battock was precipitous, and the deer could see you coming for miles! However, it was so vast that the deer, once disturbed, were likely to settle again within the marches.

Neighbouring grouse moors, Gannochy, Mill-den, Finzean and Glentanar, regarded the deer as

pests, competing with grouse and sheep for sub-
sistence, and luckily at that time the deer kept
fairly well to the Glen Dye marches. The first stag
I shot here was riddled with tick; it was not surprising that as a grouse moor, its once great value
had been extinguished.

Further, there were acres of coarse, high heather
providing little sustenance for deer, grouse or
sheep, and years of neglect in failing to make an
annual burn had obviously exacerbated the situation.

To put it politely, the place was suffering from
neglect, absentee landlordism and dilatory factor-
ing, and the income from the deer was almost
negligible.

Venison was very difficult to sell at this time,
but I realised that there was not only a market for
venison in Germany, but also that there were
foreign sportsmen anxious to start deer stalking in
Scotland.

With this in view, I contacted a Mr Spaatz of
Hamburg, and Mr Rodger, a butcher in Dundee,
to see if we could set something up. I invited Herr
Spaatz over to see the situation for himself, and
sent him out with Dowell, while I stalked with
Ferrier. I loaned Herr Spaatz my .256 Mannlicher
Schonaeur rifle, and he seemed a competent shot.
Returning in the evening, having shot a stag, I was
mortified to find that the German had missed an

easy stag at short range. I just could not understand it. Spaatz went back dispirited and our joint efforts to sell venison and attract German stalkers came to nothing. I was not well pleased when, out again three days after the German's visit, I found the stag he had fired at stone dead within two hundred yards of the firing point. It was a bad mark against Master Dowell. He should have heard the shot strike, and made a much better search.

I stalked Glen Dye quite heavily in 1958, but was not too happy with my second rifle, a Mannlicher Schonaeur .256. It was one which my father had extensively used against plains game around 1900, when he was a full-time rancher in the Orange Free State. So I asked our local gun-smith, the well known Bob Duncan of Brechin, to test it out and zero it. I then asked Bob to come stalking with me on Glen Dye. We got to within 200 yards of a good stag. The light was poor, and I did not think it was within my capabilities, so I asked Bob if he would like to try it. It fell dead to his shot, and I was more than delighted. When I congratulated him, all he said was: 'You must have forgotten. I zeroed your rifle!'

Later on that afternoon, Dowell and I espied some deer in a corrie below us, and on the far side of them, at a considerable distance, we could see the ponyman. As he moved, so did the herd, trotting smartly in our direction. I ran along a deep peat hag hoping to cut them off, but I was too far behind, and just as the last of the deer were moving across my front, I fired, still standing up, at a stag among the last ones visible. The ground was very broken with peat hags and I could only see the upper half of the beasts. I never heard the sound of a hit, and assumed I had missed. Dan Dowell and I then descended into the corrie to meet the ponyman and call it a day. The ponyman said: 'Aren't we going to collect the stag?' He had seen the beast run for fifty yards after my shot and then collapse. So we retraced our steps up the hillside to where I had fired, and 200 yards further on lay a beautiful Royal. It was a splendid climax to an interesting day.

Generally speaking, I did not at this time encourage guests to bring their women folk and I had asked Neil Findlay, factor to the Earl of Southesk at nearby Kinnaird Castle, if he would come as my guest. He said he would be delighted, and if I didn't mind, he would bring his wife. I could hardly say no, and when my wife heard this she insisted on coming too. In pique, I said she might as well bring the New Zealand 'au pair' girl too, to which she promptly agreed. So this party of five – two rifles and three female guests, set off up the glen. It was an appalling wet day and I was not in the best of humours.

I deputed Dan Dowell to take Neil and his wife

Barbara, and arranged that I would go with Nicol, the new understalker.

I had shot a stag, and the four of us (self, stalker, wife and an heir) stood absolutely soaking, impatiently waiting for Neil and party to return. At last they did, and Neil had shot the record-weighing stag on the property for the last 30 years. My immediate good humour quickly evaporated when Neil's car ran out of petrol in the glen, and I had to go into Banchory with him to get a tin of emergency supplies!

I continued to rent the Glen Dye stalking for quite a few years, as it was so convenient, but it was not really interesting stalking country, and when my business partner Noel Smart and Major Derek Foster of Park offered to take it off me if I continued as the nominee tenant, I agreed. This worked for about 10 years, and although I put in the odd day there, I left it very much to Noel and Derek, but the price of £5 per stag had risen to something like £30 at the finish.

Chapter Three

1959–61

In 1959, I felt like roaming much further afield. I decided to take Shieldaig, Gairloch, for a week, then go back to Invergarry Hotel for another week, having heard that they rented up to 10 forests!

I think the rather remote Shieldaig Hotel had been running for a year or so, but now the Strachan family had taken it over, and had rented Shieldaig Forest as bait for autumn stalkers, of whom I was one of the first. There was no regular Stalker on Shieldaig, which was part of the Gairloch Estate, but a local shepherd, Duncan McLennan, then nearly 65, had been deputed as my Stalker. The local postman, Sammy Mackenzie (Sammy the Post), seemed to have lots of time on his hands, and offered to come as pony-man/ghillie.

Shieldaig, then about 20,000 acres, was bounded by the sea on one side, by Flowerdale and Ben Eighe to the north-east, and by Ben Alligen/

Toridon on the South East. It was very picturesque, rising from sea level to nearly 3,000 feet
on Bus Bhein in three miles or so, with some steep
cliffs and precipices. Two very nice productive
brown trout lochs lay at the foot of this massif,
and entered the sea four miles to the west in Loch
Gairloch/The Minch.

It was a good four miles from the hotel to a
tin-and-wood bothy, and this we traversed in
about 90 minutes. This was really the focal point
for stalking. One could find a way up to the summit
of Bus Bhein on the west with difficulty and the
steep slopes had herds of deer on them when I
first arrived. Alternatively, it was possible to
march parallel to Bus Bhein, taking advantage of
deep peat hags and out of sight of the grazing deer,
the move to the easterly extremity of Ben Bhein,
where one could, at leisure, ascend to a ridge and,
without any mountaineering, reach the summit of
the mountain while glassing the ground below.
This was a long walk but no more strenuous in
reaching the same ridge from the west, where the
ground was really steep and often dangerous.

Duncan McLennan, Sammy and I had some very
fine stalks together, and after one excellent day
in mid-week, I asked them to join me in the bar
of the Shieldaig for a dram. We chattered away,
and they asked me if I had been in those parts
before. I told them of my time in Loch Ewe in

1940, including the incident when I had almost machine-gunned the County Council road roller. Sammy sucked his pipe, and for some minutes seemed to stare vacantly into the distance. Then he said: 'Yes, I will be remembering fine, for I was the driver of the road roller!' Of course they had both known all along who I was. They are a 'canny' lot, those Gaelic-speaking west-coasters. I enjoyed Shieldaig very much and the Strachan family ran this country hotel very well, with good food and comfortable lodgings. Then I set off for the Invergarry Hotel.

1950 must have been the zenith of renting for Captain Leslie and Mrs Bunty Hunt of the Invergarry Hotel. It was packed with stalking guests, and the forests rented included Killichonate, Glengarry, Garrygualach – Greenfield, Ardochy, Ceannaroc, and Cullachy. Ardochy had been previously owned by Edmund Luxmoore, a Darlington solicitor with whom I had been friendly as a fellow guest at Invergarry, but I think the Hydro Board were about to flood his property with a new dam, and he bought another forest near Spean Bridge, where for years he was at war with the Red Deer Commission amid much litigation, but I never grasped the ins and outs of this.

Anyway, I stalked Ardochy with Stalker Macdougal. Apart from the fact that I enjoyed it, my Game Book says little, but I do remember a glorious sight when two stags plunged into Loch Loyne in the evening, swam the loch, then trotted across my front up the hillside as the evening light was fading.

I had a nice day with McHardy, a (to me) new stalker on Glengarry. I remember he was a tough young man in his late thirties, and wore shorts. I have seen stalkers in kilts and lederhosen, but this was the only time I ever saw plain Army drill shorts! Then to Ceannaroc with Stalker MacRae, which I found rather disappointing. I had heard so much of it, and it had a reputation far above other forests which I stalked that year, but I think the Hydro Board had messed it up badly. The scenery was good, but the stalking indifferent. The few stags we saw were very wild and disturbed.

Then it was on to Culachy, and the young Stalker was Lea McNally, later to become famous as a Forest Warden, photographer and writer, but at that time hardly known. I had an excellent, most instructive time with him and killed a brace of stags on the last day of the season. Arriving back at the hotel, I found that Leslie Hunt had organised a Ghillies' Ball for all the Stalkers, ponymen, and ghillies who had been employed that season. It was a splendid gathering, and after an excellent meal, we all got down to Scottish Country Dancing.

Leslie Hunt seemed very preoccupied and in a

bad mood. I wondered why, particularly when he asked me to organise the dancing, and he departed early from the scene. Two of the ghillies had stolen two of his Land Rovers, loaded up with stags, and had disappeared into the night, and by breakfast time were being hunted by the police. It later transpired that the ghillie/thieves had recently been sacked from Inverinate Estate and Deer Forest, which at that time belonged to The Hon. Mrs Geoffrey Bowlby. There had been awful goings on there, and apart from thefts, the Rolls Royce had been set on fire and so had the Lodge! The criminals who had so upset Leslie Hunt were arrested the day after the dance by Inverness Police, but I don't know the sequel except that my Ross stalking telescope was missing.

I telephoned Lea at Cullachy in case I had lost it there – possibly left it in his Land Rover, but it could not be found. So I rang up Inverness Police at the Castle and reported it missing. The Police were able to inform me at once that they already had my telescope. It had been found in one of Leslie Hunt's stolen Land Rovers. I duly had it returned.

In August 1960 I had a young Austrian staying with me. He was then 20 and had never shot a stag. I rang up the Strachans at Shieldaig, and asked if I could rent a day. It was August and really rather too early for stalking, and in any case

I could only spare one fixed day, as I had accepted a very kind invitation from Sir Ewan and Lady Macpherson Grant to stay at Ballindalloch Castle for three days' driven-grouse shooting.

Kai Miedler and I drove across Scotland from the East Coast to the West Coast in torrential rain the whole way. Prospects for a single day looked bleak, and the Strachans had already told me that the hotel was packed, but Duncan MacLennan had very kindly agreed to let us sleep in his house, which had a tin roof.

Nearly all night the torrential rain continued

Kai (Dr Miedler), aged 20, shoots his first stag. Stalker McLenan in background. Shieldaig 1960

and the noise on the tin roof just above our heads was horrendous – just like continuous machine gun fire! Around 5 a.m. the rain stopped, and when Kai and I sat down for breakfast in the Shieldaig Hotel, the sun came out with beautiful blue skies. At 9 a.m. we marched out four miles to the loch at the foot of Bus Bhein, and as it was now very warm, out came the midges. In fifty years of stalking, I can never remember another day when the midges were so bad, but then I was always stalking in late September and October. Anyway, we survived.

We had a most exciting day but stags were scarce, and our first stalk came around 4 p.m. Duncan stalked well and got Kai close to the stags at about 120 yards. Kai fired and the stag fell. I couldn't resist the second stag and shot that as well. We were all in great spirits, and soon had the stags dragged down hill to the small loch, then boated across. We had a young ponyman with us, and soon the cavalcade was on the move down the glen, where we arrived at Shieldaig Hotel in time for supper.

After the meal, I wanted to have a conversation with Mr Strachan Sen., and arranged that Kai was to talk to the young Strachans. While Mr Strachan and I were in his private study, we heard a commotion on the Council road outside the window and Kai and young Strachan rushed in to say there had been an accident. A man was still in an overturned car in the ditch, and it was on fire. We all rushed out to help, got the driver out and quenched the fire before it really took hold. An ambulance came and took away the badly injured man. It was the road surveyor, the very one who had been embroiled in the road roller incident with Sammy Mackenzie and me many years beforehand! It is indeed a small world.

It was beginning to rain when the ambulance arrived, and this became a torrential downpour.

After all the excitement of the day, we retired for another noisy night in Duncan's spare bedroom with the loud clattering on the tin roof, but we were so tired – and elated – that we slept like logs and heard little. At breakfast time it was still raining cats and dogs, and continued thus all day. How lucky we were with that one day!

I did not need to be at Ballindalloch before 6 p.m., so we had a leisurely drive through Poolewe, Aultbea and Dundonald and called on Robert MacRae at Inverlael. He asked me to come and stalk for a day before the season ended, and this I most willingly accepted. Then we drove on to Ballindalloch, where we stayed for three days for most enjoyable grouse driving. My car was meantime full of guns and rifles and none of us realised then the ghastly Police Security Regulations that were to come into force thirty-five years later.

Later that year I stayed two nights in the Aultguish Inn, and had an excellent day with Robert. Between 1955 and 1960 the Hydro Board had driven an access road from the Garve-Braemmore Junction to Glenbeg Lodge, so that instead of having to tackle a 14-mile walk from Inverlael Lodge, one could do it in 20 minutes! From here we stalked, and I had shot two stags by midday when we stopped. Robert and his brother came to dinner with me at Aultguish that evening, and I regret to say that we all got hopelessly drunk with elation! It was a fitting end to the season.

Chapter Four

1961–66

After I failed to buy Inverlael in 1955, it had remained unsold for 2½ years. Then it was purchased by a London psychiatrist – I believe for the same price as it was offered to me. He got in touch with me, and for some years a comradely 'rapport' developed between us. He knew little of livestock farming, and had difficulty in feeding the stock he had taken over, so I was able to purchase turnips and hay for him on the East Coast and get it delivered. Hence I did not think I was asking an undue favour when I asked if I could rent the prime stalking that year. Up to that time we had only shot the odd stag, and Robert MacRae had stayed on and helped with the sheep. The doctor agreed, but said I would have to make all the arrangements myself. However, I could have the loan of Robert.

Meantime, I had accepted a lot of Robert's advice on my own equipment. As my first rifle, I bought a new BSA Mauser, fitted with a Carles Telescopic Sight – really the Rolls Royce of deer-stalking equipment at that time. Further, I bought the best stalking telescope then being made, although I still had my faithful Ross.

However, I needed much more than this. Acting on Roberts's advice, I hired three ponies from Alison, horse Trader of dingwall, for £8 each per week, complete with deer-carrying saddles and harness. I hired a Land Rover from MacRae & Dick of Inverness – land Rovers were still comparatively scarce in those days. Then I hired a ponyman, whose name I forget, but he had recently been fired from the Forestry Commission for deer poaching! He proved to be an excellent employee and very good with ponies. I installed myself in the Caledonian Hotel in Ullapool, as in the interval the Royal had been burnt down!

So with this new set-up I ventured forth for a fortnight in the best stalking period of the year – late September to mid-October.

Unlike the same period of 1955, this time the weather remained perfect for the whole time I was there. Robert was a tower of strength, and there was never any trouble with the ponies. I did invite some guests, and more then one shot his first stag there.

The whole adventure was a tremendous success, and we shot the record for over 30 years. Three incidents stand out in my memory. Normally, Robert and I and the ponyman used to ride the ponies from sea level to above 1,500 feet before we thought of glassing the slopes. However, when we set out one day, we heard a stag roar close at hand, which I shot close to the zigzag path up which we had been riding. We had left the pony-man behind to follow up later, having told him the area we proposed to stalk. It was a travelling stag and I shot it at close range practically off the footpath.

It looked an easy pick-up, but the pony would not move off the path. We had a terrible job to get it the fifty yards off the path to where the stag lay. The ground seemed quite normal if a little spongy. We had just loaded the stag on the pony's back, when the poor garron just sank, almost to its belly, in a quaking bog. Quick as a flash, Robert knifed the leather straps and we pulled the stag off the pony's back. With great difficulty, we got the pony out of the bog without damage. It could easily have broken a leg. Once we had got the pony to the path, we hauled the stag to where it stood and loaded it there. The pony must have 'smelt' the bog; it was not obvious to us. We had been very lucky.

On another occasion, Commander Colin Keay, a great naval chum of mine, was a guest, so I sent him out with Robert. I also had Duncan

Mackenzie as another guest. Duncan was Secretary of Angus National Farmers Union, and had seen war service in the Seaforth Highlanders, got a commission and served in Persia (now Iran), where he had married a nursing officer from the U.K. He was born in Wester Ross. I had a superb collection of rifles in my Land Rover, ranging from my brand new BSA Mauser .270 to the Winchester Springfield .30 cal with sniper sight and the Mannlicher .256 already mentioned as having been zeroed by Bob Duncan. However, in spite of my advice to the contrary, Duncan insisted on bringing his own rifle, obviously 'looted' post-war, which was a Drilling, a double sixteen-bore with something like a .280 single barrel, single shot, mounted above. It weighed half a ton and was totally unsuitable for Red Deer stalking in the Highlands, but Duncan was adamant. It was his prized possession, and he wanted to 'blood' it. As I was to be Duncan's stalker, there was too much gear to carry, and I left my own rifle behind.

Having spied a good herd of deer grazing along the Rappach Water not far from the Rhidorroch March, we managed to get into a perfect position. The wind was O.K., and the herd came on steadily, slowly towards us. There were at least five good shootable stags in this large herd, and I pointed out a Royal to Duncan and told him to shoot when he was ready. There was no hurry, and the weather was perfect. Duncan fired and missed at a range of under one hundred yards. I told him to reload and shoot again, but the awful Drilling contraption, unlike a magazine rifle, took ages to open, extract the empty and place in a 'full', and the whole herd was off. A great chance had been lost.

On the last day of my 'let' the wind was doing strange things, and we were not certain of its direction by the time we reached 1,500 feet. I told the ponyman to wait and follow us as best he could. As Robert and I ascended the high ridge – I had no guests that day – we found all the deer in a different glen, and decided to stalk this, and not the glen we had discussed with the ponyman. We had some excellent stalking, and I shot three stags by 3 p.m. The trouble now was to acquaint the ponyman with our changed plans.

That ponyman was possibly the best I ever had the pleasure of meeting. He was very intelligent and sharp-witted. Not only had he glassed us crossing the ridge, but correctly anticipated the line of action we might take. When Robert and I had glassed the last stag, we spied not only the ponyman below us at the bottom of our glen, but the three ponies and Land Rover! he had moved the lot, and I don't think he even had a driving licence! We met him halfway up the glen, and in no time we had loaded a stag on each of the three ponies and were homeward bound. Not only was it the end of a perfect day, but a perfect fortnight.

When I was stalking alone with Robert, we had the most perfect understanding of one another. On one occasion we spotted a lone stag sunbathing in a peat hag, at a range of about 180 yards. I told Robert I didn't think I would hit a lying stag at that range. He replied, 'If you miss it, it will rise and give you five seconds for another shot, and this time you will get it.' This is exactly what did happen. On another occasion we were returning quite late in the afternoon, and it was the only day we had dense fog on the high tops. We knew there were stags in front of us because of the roaring, but were certain they would see us before we saw them, so we silently advanced on the roaring. Like a flash, the dense fog suddenly cleared, and there, one hundred yards in front of us, was a big herd of deer with seven shootable stags. Robert was leading, six feet ahead of me, and he stopped – rigid. I put my rifle over his shoulder and whispered 'Stop breathing!' At that moment I fired, and a stag fell dead!

Robert, then aged about 25, was one of the finest, if not *the* finest, stalker I ever met. He taught me a great deal, although I was fifteen years older than he.

Although Robert and I were very great friends

and he got married and settled at Elphin near Ullapool, we never managed to stalk together again. He died before he reached the age of 35 in very sad circumstances.

The owner of Inverlael never really forgave me, and was very jealous of our achievement. We never spoke again after I said goodbye to him. He is now dead and the estate was on the market in 1997 for £626,000. To me Inverlael will always remain my favourite deer forest of the over 50 I have stalked. It has a bit of everything.

Glendye 1962–63

In 1962 I had a serious car crash coming back from the Lairg Sheep Sales, where I had bought and sold quite a number of beasts, and in 1963 I got married, which put a brake on widespread stalking. Notwithstanding, I put in a few days in both seasons at nearby Glendye, but the results were not spectacular. One beautiful sunny day with no wind and very long visibility, I was having my packed lunch on Cloch-na-Bhein, when Dan Dowell remarked it was a hopeless day. Did I think it feasible to burn some of the very coarse long heather, which provided no food for grouse, deer or sheep, and I suggested we started a small fire. This Dan and I worked at hard, while the ghillie sat idly on a rock telling us what to do. Sadly, that was the way Glendye was run in those days.

On another occasion I was out all day for one stag, with my farm manager, Bert Hay. I think we were probably accompanied by Nicol, who was a good competent stalker. Dan Dowell had some business away from the estate, and was not out that day. Motoring home, I stopped at the summit of Cairn o' Mounth to admire the view and got out of the car. I heard a stag roar far out on Melunchart, and leaving the car there, we set off to stalk. After a mile or so, we spotted the roaring stag, who had gathered some hinds in a sheltered glade in the valley, and the final stalk in was not too difficult. I told Bert he could take my rifle and shoot. He was quite a good shot – ex-Scots Guards – and the stag was well shot through the heart. It was then that I discovered Bert and I had left our knives in the car. How were we to gralloch the stag? Well, we did succeed, even if it was rather an untidy job, using a .280 pointed bullet. I had laid down my Ross telescope, stick and haversack, when I got down to the gralloch. We hauled the stag to a peat covered knoll and I left my stick to mark the spot with a white handkerchief attached to the crook. Then we set off back to the car, some four miles distant. Dan Dowell had returned from Fettercairn, and breasting the

Cairn o' Mounth, came on my abandoned car, which he recognised. He waited for us.

I asked him to recover the stag next day and collect my stick, haversack and stalking telescope, all of which I had left with the stag when we hastened back to the car, as the light was failing and I did not fancy a long walk over very broken ground in bad light. Well, the stag, my stick and the haversack were all collected; some time later I picked them up at Dan's house, but the Ross telescope was nowhere to be found. I always reckoned that one of the summer students, recruited for the stalking season, had stolen it. It was really a great loss.

Invergarry 1964

The Invergarry Hotel was still going strong, with an impressive list of rented forests. So I determined to go back there and try my luck again. My first day was on Invergarry North with Jock McAskill. He was a wonderful stalker and leader and got me in superbly to a nice 11 pointer with 20 hinds.

Next day I was off to Ceannaroc. Leslie Hunt said I would have to stalk alone, but at the last moment he produced a 55-year-old man called Martin, who would also drive Leslie's Land Rover. We arrived on a high mountain track, and fog was dense. Martin said he knew the ground, and we set off in the direction of some roaring, which soon stopped. However we kept marching on and on. I suspected Martin had lost his way, and I said so. He became pretty grumpy. Half an hour later I knew he had lost his way. We were going round in a circle. I was wearing new boots, only just purchased that year at Berchtesgaden, and I found my previous imprints. They could belong to no one else. Now I was very grumpy. I said if the fog did not clear, I would take the first burn we came to, and keep descending until it ran into a loch or river, downhill all the way. Luckily, the fog then cleared. Ascending to my records, I shot a stag, but the home coming was decidedly frosty.

I complained to Leslie Hunt. Next day he sent me out with Martin Jun., son of the other Martin, and I could tell from the start we were not going to get on. This Martin was a professional Stalker, and had the South Invergarry Beat. He tried to kill me by the pace he set off. It was very steep, and by the time I was on the highest ridge, I was almost exhausted. There was no need for this haste. We had plenty of time walking along the ridges, and there were plenty of stags below us. I shot a stag and then we went home. There was little repartee between us. He was obviously hostile because of the previous day.

Chapter 5

1965–73

This was really the last year I stalked Glendye with much vigour, but I did have some good days with Nicoll, the Second Stalker. He was a very big man, about six foot three, and powerfully built. He was a good stalker, and a great 'dragger'. I don't think he ever got the chance to show off his quality, and soon he left Glendye for good and became foreman of the Tay Fisheries Netting Station at Lunan Bay.

That season I was invited by the Earl of Airlie, through his excellent factor David Laird, to have a day at Glendoll at the head of Glencova. Glendoll came under the Head Stalker at Rottal, Sandy Mearns, where I was told to report and pick up the Glendoll Stalker, Charlie Oswald, whom I had never met before. Charlie was a hardy hill man, about the same age as me, and had been a tail gunner in Bomber Command in World War II.

I had never been near Glendoll before, and we

passed the Glenclova Hotel, then up a Council tarmac road to Braedownie, a sheep farm. Thereafter it was Forestry Commission tracks into Glendoll Forest, which Lord Airlie rented from F.C.

We came to the famous Jock's Road, which leads from Glenclova, Glendoll, over the high mountains and emerges on the Glenshee road after passing through Glencallater. I had read about Jock's road before, as a few years previously five hikers, making their way from Braemar through Glencallater, had lost their bearings and their lives on the watershed coming into Glendoll. They were found only when the deep snow had melted.

Anyway, Charlie and I followed the path up to a shelter near where the hikers had perished. Then we cut right and landed on the top of Craig Mellon, nearly 3,000 ft. It was lunch time and I was opening my dirty wartime gas mask haversack, which contained my ready-mixed tea, sugar, and milk and sandwiches, when Charlie produced a magnificent lunch basket with two thermos flasks, and said 'Will you have Indian or China, sir.' I was quite flabbergasted, and will remember this to my dying day! We had a good picnic lunch together, then started to stalk. The sides of Craig Mellon are very steep and there are several dangerous precipices, but with care, the whole face is stalked, except a vertical cliff near the old Glendoll Lodge, now a Youth Hostel.

*The steepness of Craig Mellon in Glendoll, 1979. John Baynes,
Head Stalker with MFG's stag*

Charlie had verbal diarrhoea. He never stopped
talking *until* he could smell deer, and then he shut
up like a clam. He was a very good stalker, and
both his brothers were well known Head Keepers/
Stalkers – Ben Alder and Glentanar. We parted
great friends, and I said I hoped Lord Airlie would
ask me again. I had shot one or two stags.

1966 *Dalnarcardoch & Glendoll*

In the summer of 1966, Michael Yardley, who had set up a gunshop in Brechin, told me he could sub-let deer stalking on Dalcardoch Forest, between Blair Atholl and Dalwhinnie. It belonged to Major Richard Pilkington of the famous glass-making family. I already knew Dick slightly, as thirty years previously he had courted my aunt, Rosa Forsyth-Grant, in our native village of St Cyrus!

Dalnacardoch was then about 30,000 acres, and was shaped like a boot. The sole of the 'boot' ran along the north side of the A9 between Dalnamein and Drumochter, and was several miles in length. Near the 'toe', Dalnaspidal was opposite. The 'leg' was several miles long, and ran up a track suitable for 4 x 4 vehicles to Sronfadrig Lodge, and a mile beyond that was the Forest of Gaick. To the east, the ground was fairly flat where it marches with Dalnamein and is quite good grouse moor, but to the north and west the ground is dotted with high hills and deep semi-precipitous corries. In 1965, the average bag was 1,000 brace of grouse, walked up, and 150 stags. The latter must have been three times the sustainable average, and I can only assume that the surplus came from adjacent under-stalked forests. In 1966, the Head Stalker was Alistair McGregor, and the Second Stalker,

Rex McCullough, spent the stalking season at
Sronfadrig. His brother was Head Stalker of Glen-
bruar – a post he held for some 40 years into the
nineties. Dalnacardoch Lodge was most dilapidated. Dick Pilkington had plenty of money, but
would not spend a penny on the old lodge. He
had married a German lady after the war, and they
had one child – very handicapped. I liked Dick
very much but he was eccentric. To say that his
wife Hilda was eccentric would be an under-
statement.

For the next seven or eight years I stalked
Dalnacardoch as hard as I had ever stalked Glendye. Alastair McGregor and Rex McCullough
were both good stalkers, but hated each other's
guts and were always at war. Somehow Dick and
Hilda Pilkington seemed to pour oil on the fire!
I always tried to be strictly neutral and non-com-
mittal.

About 1968 Alastair McGregor had suffered
enough and retired to Perth. At Hilda's instiga-
tion, Rex became Head Stalker. Sometimes, if they
were short of stalkers, they impressed Hugh
McLaughlan, who was the Sheep Farm Manager
for the Duke of Atholl. He too was a competent
stalker and knew the ground well. I shot a lot of
stags at Dalnacardoch, but will not bore the reader
with repetition. All the same, some stalks do stand
out.

On one occasion, I was just a 'camp follower'. Alastair McGregor was stalking for my guest Kai Miedler. He got him in very well to a good 11 pointer and fired. There was a loud click! The unfired cartridge had stuck in the breach, and maybe the extractors on the bolt of the old .256 Mannlicher were worn. Then I remembered this 70-year-old rifle had a ramrod in the stock, removable by taking aside the heel plate.

Alastair, Kai and I crawled back another 30 yards out of sight of the deer, assembled the three-piece ramrod, ejected the cartridge and fitted another. Kai and Alastair then moved in undetected and shot the stag.

Sadly Dick died during my forays at Dalnacardoch and Hilda was in charge. Arriving there one dark October evening, Hilda told me to go and stay at Sronfadrig – a ponyman would be up in the morning with food. Rex was away at a court case, and would not be back till noon the following day. Now Sronfadrig had no electricity and was as cold as charity. I found the key in the gutter, and entered the dilapidated old lodge. I managed to get some light – torches or mini-gas. I took my rifle to bed with me. It was dark, cold, spooky and I needed all my nerve! Around 1 a.m. I saw headlights coming up the glen, and wondered if it was bandits coming to loot the place. I slipped a cartridge into the breech of my rifle. I need not have worried. Rex had got back earlier than expected, and I stayed with him for a week.

One morning, around 5 a.m., we set off in the pitch dark to ascend a high mountain on the Gaick march. Stupidly I stumbled and fell into the mini-river at the very start, but we continued on. By sunrise we were on top of the mountain, with magnificent views to the west down the steep slopes towards Dalnacardoch Lodge, and there were plenty of stags on the slopes below us. We stalked a big herd, and shot three out of it. Now we had to get them down to the glen below us.

Sid Fender, a retired Blairgowrie Police Inspector, was the ponyman, and had instructions to walk three ponies up the glen once the light was good enough to see what we were doing. Rex was a very strong lad, and said he would manage to drag down two stags if I could manage one.

The hillside was very steep with lots of scree and I was afraid we might get pulled on to moving scree by the stag, and crash down over several rocks to the floor of the glen. Meantime, Sid had spotted us, and Rex waved him to get below us. I warned Rex that this was most dangerous. The stags could crash down out of control, or dislodge rocks, which would descend on Sid and the ponies. This is just what happened. A huge boulder got dislodged and careered downhill. It weighed about two cwts. It passed between Sid and the leading pony. It was lucky it did not hit the leading pony. Any person or pony hit by it would have been pulped.

After this, we got the three stags to the floor of the glen, and Rex departed with a rather startled Sid down to Sronfadrig with three loaded saddles.

I was lucky in really having the run of Dalna-cardoch for a few years, and asked up quite a few guests, including Dr Kai Miedler and Captain James Branscome, U.S.N., whom I had met in the Navy.

We always stayed in the Tilt or Blair Atholl Hotel in the village, but sometimes I was alone and longed for female company. I rang up the boss of an Escort Agency in Charing Cross Road, London, and asked if he could send me up a girl for two or three nights. Debbie, whom I had never met, duly arrived at Blair Atholl Station off the Euston/Inverness day express, and we adjourned to the hotel for the evening. She was ill-equipped for the Highlands. Snow was falling outside. In the morning, instead of rushing off to Sronfadrig, I took her to Macphersons of Pitlochry and kitted her out as a true Scottish lairdess! Then we set off to Sronfadrig, arriving about 2 p.m. Just after 3.30 we had climbed one of the bigger hills and started stalking, Rex in charge.

I certainly shot one stag. Maybe Rex shot an-other. Rex then said he would take Debbie, who was shaking with cold and had frozen snow sticking to her clothes, and he wanted me to wait for the ponyman and help load the stags. To this I agreed, and in due course Hamish arrived and we reached Sronfadrig with full saddles. Meantime Rex had prepared a bath for Debbie, and from what I heard later, I think he shared it with her!

Thereafter we had a terrific meal and a skinful of Scotch at Sronfadrig, and reached Blair Atholl in time to be locked out of the hotel. We got in at last, had a super night, and Debbie left for London next day. Expensive? Yes, but so is stalking!

At one stage I had a party staying at Blair Atholl – Kai, his brother-in-law, and their wives, and we could not really stalk three rifles. Rex told me to ring Colonel Hornung at Dalnaspidal Lodge and ask if we could rent a beat for a day or two, and thither I went. I found Colonel Hornung a charming old man of nearly 80, and his fellow guest, Air Marshal Sir Thomas Elmhirst. He had been one of the six survivors – I think 23 perished – from the disastrous food poisoning at Loch Maree Hotel in the 1920s. He told me the whole story and I wish I could have recorded it on tape. It was talked about for the next 50 years.

I had a nice day with Stalker Kennedy on Dalnaspidal and the Colonel very kindly asked me back. This I naturally accepted for another season.

1967 *Glendoll and Greenhill*

I had several days on Glendoll and the Greenhill – all part of the same Airlie Estate Glendoll Beat, with Charlie Oswald.

Although I was only too pleased to pay for my sport, Lord Airlie would not hear of it, and I stalked there for several years without ever paying a penny in rent.

Kai Miedler and I stayed at the Jubilee Arms at Dykehead, Cortachy, when we were stalking Glendoll for more than a day. It was an ideal pub for field sportsmen, very well run by John Duguid and his wife.

Charlie Oswald had a new youth as a ghillie, George Miller, and on this occasion he decided to take Kai Miedler as his 'Rifle' and arranged for George to stalk for me – the first time he had ever been 'the Stalker'.

George and I pounded up Jock's Road to 'the Shelter', cut right for the ascent to the Craig Mellon plateau, from which we could glass the great long sides of the valley down below. By 3 p.m. we had shot a stag and hauled it down to Jock's Road – not a difficult task because the slopes were so steep. George was most elated, and wondered if we could get a second stag. This entailed climbing up to the Shelter again on Jock's Road, which would take at least one and a half hours, then traversing the plateau of Craig Mellon towards Glendoll Lodge, as we had disturbed the whole of the Upper Glen. Although I was nearing 50, I fell for this marathon.

Far down the glen, we spied two lots of deer and were stalking one of them, and I shot a good ten-pointer. George was over the moon. First time out as a stalker, he had scored twice! We met Charlie Oswald and Kai where the Esk and Whitewater meet. They had been on the Greenhill, and had had a blank day. This was very bad luck. You could not get a better, more knowledgable stalker than Charlie Oswald, and the Greenhill marches with Invermark, one of the best deer forests in Scotland, but if the wind is wrong, there is little that can be done about it. I tried to play down George's great success to console poor Charlie.

I had some very nice stalks with Charlie on the Greenhill. Usually we left the car at the Clova Hotel, and climbed up to Loch Brandy, and then the high plateau above it. It was well over 2,500 feet. We often saw excellent herds, but I was no longer interested in trophies, and we just shot out the poorer quality stags.

Charlie was a collector of weapons and had a

great collection. This was when the 'Troubles' in Northern Ireland were just starting, and sadly a police search on Charlie's house – probably a tip-off – resulted in finding an illegal submachine gun. As a result Charlie lost his job. Thus in 1968 the stalking at Glendoll was out, but I had a very nice day from Rottal Lodge with Head Stalker Sandy Mearns in Glen Moy, where I shot two stags after two long belly-crawl stalks which I remember very well. Sandy was a big man but an excellent Stalker, who knew his ground well. Glen Moy was difficult terrain – more grouse moor than deer forest – and a lot of crawling had to be done. I made up for lost days at Glendoll by many more days at Dalnacardoch, where Dick Pilkington had died, and his wife had promptly got rid of Alastair McGregor (who retired to Perth) and put Rex McCullough in charge.

I needed a change of scenery in 1969, and took a week at Alvie, near Newtonmore, which belonged to Fergus Williamson. Fergus had been a midshipman with me in 1940 in Scapa Flow and it was interesting to meet him again and his charming wife, whose maiden name sounded most aristocratic: 'McMurrough Kavannah'!

One day I set off with Head Stalker Thomson and his assistant. We must have left the assistant and ponyman far behind in the glen, and after a very long hike I shot a stag. Stalker Thomson said it would be a long time before the ponyman caught up with us, and as it was raining, suggested I should retrace my steps down the path and wait for him where I had left my lunch and other equipment in the estate Land Rover. This I did, and I knew I would have to wait at least two hours.

I was not idle, as I continually glassed the hills and surrounding terrain. I spotted a large travelling stag coming my way out of a mature pine plantation, and in a flash I abandoned the Land Rover with my rifle, and tried to ambush the beast. On and on it came, and I had plenty of cover among the large mature pine trees. The stag stopped for a few seconds at a range of about one hundred yards, and I killed it with my first shot. By the time Thomson arrived with my first stag, I had gralloched the second, and it was loaded into the Rover in no time. Thomson never made any spectacular comment on any of this and when we arrived at Alvie Lodge, I just had time to leave an invitation for Fergus and his wife to dine with me in Newtonmore the next evening. Next morning I met Mrs Williamson, who told me Fergus had left early for London, but that she would be delighted to dine with me at the Balavil Arms Hotel in Newtonmore that evening.

Mrs Williamson and I met in the evening, had a pleasant dinner, and she departed. I cannot really recollect much more of the sporting side of Alvie, but when Fergus returned from London, his attitude seemed quite frosty. I never discovered whether it had something to do with my second stag or because I had taken his wife out for dinner alone! The mystery and frostiness persisted until his death some years later.

1970 *Abernethy* (*Forest Lodge, Nethybridge.*)

Always searching for new territory, I discovered Forest Lodge was available for that season. The Lodge lies in the foothills of the Cairngorms, and the southernmost top of the march is on Cairngorm. After a good warm-up on Dalnacardoch, I set out for Grantown-on-Spey with my two guests, Jim Branscome, late of U.S. Navy, and Dr Kai Miedler, with both of whom I had done much stalking in the past. We set up H.Q. in the Palace Hotel, Grantown, where we took two adjacent suites and were treated like Royalty!

Charlie Robertson, who was well known in the Atholl country, was the Stalker here, and the estate was owned by the Naylor Brothers (Far East Shipping family). It was reputed the Naylors were selling the whole estate to RSPB, which indeed they did after our let. It was a fairly big forest, with huge conifer plantations on the low ground, and it sloped up to Bynack Mor and Bynack Beg, and eventually to Cairn Gorm at 4,000 feet. It was fairly well stocked, and Charlie Robertson was an able Stalker, then probably in his early 50s.

We shot quite a few stags, and one day was memorable. Charlie allowed me to act as Stalker, and I set off with Kai Miedler, while Charlie took Jim Branscome. After a long hike, I spied a nice Royal, not far from the summit of Bynack Mor. We got into position 150 yards from the lone stag, who was lying and enjoying a sunbathe. It looked an easy shot. After 30 minutes, with the stag sleeping in the sun, I decided to shoot it lying. The light was good, and it was not a difficult target. I missed it clean, and it leapt to its feet and in a trice had disappeared at the gallop over the summit of Bynack Mor.

I was disgusted with myself, and whenever I see Byneck Mor from the Tomintoul-Grantown highway, I still feel the same awful feeling of depression!

Nigel Grant was a well known 'mine host' at Grantown, and we were treated with great reverence (I don't know why!) by his manager and head waitress. Jim had to return to USA, but before I put him on the London Night Express at Aviemore, I took him for a day tour of Wester Ross, including Inverewe Gardens. Kai and I decided we needed female company in the evening, so while I went west to Gairloch, he took my Land Rover to Montrose and picked up two bar girls who were old friends of ours. One was a single mother with a child of one year, which she also brought along. When I got back to the hotel from Aviemore, Kai was already installed in our suites, with pram and accessories but no luggage. Our revered status vanished! The head waitress regarded Maggie and Isobel with disdain until I made up a fictitious name and Isobel became The Hon. Isobel Kidd, Lord Cairngorm's daughter. I only hoped that no such people existed in real life!

The stalking went on and the girls enjoyed themselves by day in Grantown-on-Spey and neighbourhood. I must confess, the hectic life took toll of our energy and marksmanship, and one day Charlie caustically remarked: 'If yer wud leave them hinds alone in Inverness at night, you wud dae better wi the stags by day!' Anyway, a good time was had by all, and we got on very well with Charlie and parted the best of friends.

The following year I hammered away at Dalnacardoch and Glendoll with reasonable results. George Miller was then the Stalker.

In August 1972 I had an invitation to shoot driven grouse from the Earl of Strathmore, but he was too ill to leave Glamis himself and sadly died while I was staying at Holwick Lodge on the Yorkshire-Durham border. After some excellent shooting, we packed up in reverence to his death.

Albie (Hon. M.A. Bowes Lyon) was acting as our host, and about eight shooting guests were living in the lodge. At breakfast, when Albie announced his Lordship's death overnight, we were all bidden to the funeral at Glamis Castle, to be held five days later. It was a sad end to some very pleasant days. The London Agent for the Strathmore Estate in Yorkshire was Alastair Turnbull, whom I well knew from former visits, and he had never shot a stag. I knew Timothy (the late Earl) would not be offended if I took Alastair to shoot his first stag and bury the Earl the same day.

Alastair arrived off the train one evening, stayed overnight with me, and at 8 a.m. we set out to stalk on Hunthill in Angus. David Wilson was appointed as our stalker. Alastair was 'the rifle', and I just accompanied them. By 12.30 Alastair had shot his first stag, and was most ceremoniously blooded. Then it was off the hill at full speed to get washed and changed into full-dress funeral clothes, Alastair being one of the main pall bearers.

We knew that the funeral would be a big affair, and the Queen Mother was certain to be there. We had not counted on the Monarch also being present. We arrived in excellent time, being only the second guests to arrive. Alastair was whisked away, and the police told me to leave my car where it was – right opposite the main entrance to the Castle. I was horrified. My rifle was in the car, telescopes and walkie-talkies were on the back window ledge, and there were still bloodstains on the car! I wanted to park it far away but the police were adamant – 'Leave it where it is!'

I was then offered a place on a garden seat next to Sir Joseph Nickerson, the famous game shot and farm seedsman, who was tenant of Strathmore Grouse Moor of international repute – Wemmergill.

I knew Joe Nickerson from former times, and when he offered me a place to the kirk in his Rolls, I jumped at the kind offer. I could leave my bloodstained, heavily armed 'beroosh' where it stood! Joe brought me back to the Castle and went on to tea with the Monarch and Queen Mother, but I made my excuses and left in my car like a scalded cat! Luckily the police did not intervene!

Chapter six

1973-75

After Lord Strathmore's funeral and Alastair's first stag in 1972, I had a marathon stalking season. First at Lord Dalhousie's magnificent retreat, Invermark, in Angus – one of the most productive forests in Scotland. There is not much very steep ground, but some very picturesque landscapes and waterfalls. Head Stalker Bert Osler deputed Jim Watson as my Stalker, and I shot four stags in one day, but nothing spectacular. Then to Glendoll for a good warm-up.

Needing new territory, I spotted an advertisement for Balmore and Glencannich in Inverness-shire, and hither I went, to stay at the Glenaffric Hotel, Glencannich, where mine host was none other then Murdo Mackenzie, who had been one of my officers in HMS *Montrose* at the Coronation Review in 1953. He ran an excellent pub with good food and plenty of hot water! Then I set off to see what I had rented, and the Stalker (so called) met Kai and me on the Monday morning. The Stalker was really a shepherd on the Balmore Grazings and was about the least desirable I ever encountered. His assistant was quite different – Colin Hendry, a youth about 19, whose father was a most renowned Stalker/teacher on Rhum. We took our vehicles to the Loch Mullardoch dam, and parked by the Sluices, meeting a bunch of Arabs who had rented Inverinate, which marched with out territory. The ground I had rented ran roughly up the road from Glencannich and was rightly described in Whitehead's book as 'sheep grazing', frequented occasionally by deer. This was a very apt description. The grazings were fairly flat, but at the foot of the Mullardoch Dam, the ground rose rapidly to Sgur na Lapaig, over 3,000 feet, and fronted on Loch Mullerdoch where the estate had a boat. The owner of the estate, an absentee baronet from the Bristol area, also had the rights on Fasnakyle, across the Council Road at the foot of Loch Mullardoch, running roughly parallel to the Balmore Grazings. This was pretty steep and suitable ground, and judging by the roaring, had a fair population of deer.

Kai and I usually split up, one going with the Shepherd Stalker, and one with Colin Hendry. Colin was a knowledgeable and very pleasant young man, and seemed pretty capable – quite the reverse of his senior!

We did shoot a number of stags – usually very scarce on the Balmore side, and one day Kai and I decided to share a rifle with the Stalker/ Shepherd. Well into the forest and not far from the Balmore march, the three of us closed a bunch of five stags. The Head Stalker really made a mess of getting in – too fast and too much noise, and at 150 yards range the stags moved out at a trot. They were not easy targets, and I had the rifle. I did not think I would shoot successfully and let them go. The Stalker was quite rude and said I should have taken them on the trot. I disagreed, as the ground was very broken, with peat hags, and the target was far from steady. I think we eventually got a stag, and the noise cleared the area, so I suggested we had a pause while Kai and I climbed to the top of Sgur na Lapaig. The Stalker would not hear of this, and said he would summon the pony and load the stag, so I told him I would leave Kai with him to help, and I would stalk downhill all the way to the boat on Loch Mullardoch, where we arranged a rendezvous with pony and stag.

Halfway down to Loch Mullardoch, I spied a herd of deer, including a good shootable stag, grazing on a knoll in the shallow valley that finally led to the loch, and I decided to stalk them. I got within two hundred and fifty yards in pretty flat ground, and some of the hinds became very suspicious. It took me a long time to make a further 50 yards and I thought another move and the hinds would be off. I decided to fire at the stag – range about 250 yards. I fired, and the hinds made off. The stag never moved. I reloaded quickly and fired again. This time the stag fell to the shot. I went up to examine him. Both bullets had been mortal. That was presumably why the stag never moved after the first shot. There was only about 1½ inches between the two bullet holes, and I was delighted, as I never considered myself anything but below average as a rifle shot. I gralloched the stag, and saw that the main party had heard the shot and was coming towards me.

I received no congratulations from the so-called Head Stalker. He commented, 'If you could shoot at that range, why waste my time in not shooting the morning stag that you let go some two hours earlier?' We trudged down to the loch and loaded the stag into the boat in a very frosty atmosphere.

Towards the end of my let, I had to go to Fort William on business, and left Kai to stalk Fasnakyle on his own. He shot a stag and was back at the hotel by 2 p.m. and told me that once he had shot the stag, the stalker had said, 'That's it,' and packed up, in spite of a lot of other beats in the area, and we were well down on the promised numbers.

We left Balmore/Fasnakyle in a bad temper. It

was the worst forest let I had ever had, and the Stalker/Shepherd was the last straw. The only consolation was the excellent hotel.

Colin Hendry, following his father's footsteps, went on to become a well known 'Head' in Ross-shire. I am sure he would have been a great success, and was still there 26 years later. My lawyers conducted an acrimonious correspondence with the landowner, and I think I received some cash compensation. The ill feeling did not stop there. I met the son of the baronet in Bristol after his father had died and neither he nor I enjoyed each other's company!

In 1973, I concentrated my efforts on Dalnacardoch and Glendoll. Rex McCullough was out of favour with Mrs Pilkington at Dalnacardoch, and there was a replacement for MacGregor, but I sensed that Hilda Pilkington had something up her sleeve. The replacement was Ben Fernie, an ex-Royal Marine, very fit and keen to learn. Rex McCullough had damaged his back or his ankle, and Ben was looking after another guest of the estate at the bottom of the glen. Rex said I would have to stalk on my own. Out of the kitchen window of Sronfadrig Lodge, we could see a good herd of deer near the summit of the big round hill opposite. Rex told me the route to take, and said that he would watch me from the kitchen window and direct me with my very crude 'walkie-talkie', bought in my ex-Government Stores Shop in London's Strand. Of course these were really unlicensed and illegal, but cheap.

I set off to ascend the mountain, but when I was well up I could not see the deer. I called Rex for instructions. 'They're guy close ahead of you' said Rex, 'and keep yer bloody arse doon.' As soon as I saw the deer, a sharp snow flurry drove them a hundred yards directly below me. The mountain was round and the wind swept round both sides of the circular top in such a way that the contrary air currents, full of snow, kept meeting right above the herd, and sometimes the down-draught sent the snow cascading over the herd and down to the valley below. The snow was quite thick, and kept fogging up my telescopic sight. There were two or three good shootable stags, and all I wanted was a break in the snow storm to open fire. The wind played awful tricks, and suddenly I noticed that the snow around me was blowing over the herd. In a trice they had my wind and were off like rockets. I never got a shot.

On the R.T. I tried to tell Rex the sorry tale, but it so happened I must have been on the same wave as a fleet of Polish trawlers fishing in the Minch, and Rex could not hear me for the chattering between the ships. Suddenly he could stand it no longer and bawled into the R.T. 'Shut up yer Polish bastards and let's get a word in.' Sadly it had no effect. I doubt if the Poles could understand English. I only hoped the Post Office Licence Enforcers were not listening in.

Having had quite a successful time at Dalnacardoch, I moved on to Glendoll when Kai arrived from Austria, and we stayed at the Jubilee Arms at Dykehead in Angus. It was an ideal pub for stalkers.

At Glendoll there was a new Stalker, Ian Holmes, who told me he came from Kinlochewe. I had him placed immediately, as I had known his father, who owned Kinlochewe Estate before he sold it to Willie Whitbread, the Brewer, who owned the massive stalking fronting Loch Maree and including Ardlair, a large forest on its own.

Ian did not know Glendoll. It was his first season but he was a very tough young man in his twenties then, and very enthusiastic. We were on top of Craig Mellon, when we were hit first by very heavy snow, then fog. Just before visibility closed down, I shot a good stag and was quite glad to call it a day. Not so Ian, who was driven on by all the roaring stags close to us but invisible in the fog. We spent about ninety minutes chasing them in the fog, but they always saw us before we saw them. Then we decided to leave the summit of Craig Mellon and make for Jock's Road, nearly 3,000 feet below us. This particular area of Craig Mellon is the steepest. The wet snow was ankle deep. We started dragging the stag, but I could hardly keep my feet on the steep slopes. I tried tobogganing on my bottom. This was even worse. Once started, I couldn't stop. There was a great danger of falling over the precipice. Ian also found the going very hard. The carcase was also tobogganing on the steep slopes, and raced out of control. I shouted to Ian to let go as I lost my balance. Ian let go and the carcase shot over a precipice and crashed into a Rowan tree over a hundred yards below. By the time we reached it, it was like pulp, with every bone broken. I was really 'all in' by this time, soaked right through and freezing. I think we left the carcase where it was and did our best to descend. The fog and snow were still with us.

Meanwhile Kai had been stalking on the other side of the hill near the march with Moulzic – part of Balmoral Deer Forest. I called him up on the 'walkie-talkie' and was lucky to get him. I told him I was nearly exhausted, and asked if he could get the Land Rover as far up Jock's Road as he could and wait for us. We made it, but I literally fell into the seat of the Land Rover, totally exhausted, soaking wet and frozen stiff. Kai drove down the glen, dropping Ian off at his house, then down to the Jubilee Arms, during which time I polished off a full half bottle of Scotch! Kai ran a bath for me and after thawing out, I felt a lot better. I fully expected pneumonia at worst, a cold at least. However, strangely enough, next day I was perfectly fit again with no ill effects.

In 1976 my old stalking friend Jim Branscome from the USA was scheduled to accompany me. Kai had already joined me at the Tilt Hotel in Blair Atholl, where we intended having a warm-up at Dalnacardoch before going further west. Jim, having retired as Captain USN, was also a Doctor of Explosives and worked for the US Government. One evening the US Embassy in London rang us at the hotel to say Jim's wife had been killed – broken neck – in a riding accident in USA and would not now be coming. To my astonishment, Jim rang me next day from London and said he was catching the Euston/Inverness night train, stopping at Blair Atholl, and would be with us next morning in time for stalking.

Meantime, I received an invitation from Col. Leslie Gray Cheape to stalk on his Glenaladale Forest beside Bonnie Prince Charlie's monument at Glenfinnan. So I fixed Kai and Jim to stalk for two to three days via Invergarry Hotel, and we arranged to rendezvous four days later at the Spean Bridge Hotel. I motored south on the road to Fort William, then took the Mallaig road via Corpach, and 300 yards from the Monument turned left into Leslie's short drive up to his Lodge, which was a new Colt Bungalow.

A local friend of mine, much younger and fitter, had told me what hard work Glenaladale was, but from the data in Whitehead's book, the highest ground was well under 2,800 feet from Loch Shiel and I felt I could easily tackle it.

I set off down Loch Shiel with the stalker Bob Crockart in Leslie's launch, and we landed well down the loch and moored the boat. We then had to climb the hills. It was the toughest climb I ever encountered. The ground was very wet and boggy. There were no paths. We sank to the ankles in gooey peat at each step upwards. No wonder my young friend had complained of the hard work!

We finally reached the summit of the local range, where we had wonderful views down Loch Shiel. Deer were not numerous, and once on the top, stalking was not too difficult. I much enjoyed my stay and seeing a new forest, and Leslie and his wife were most lavish with their hospitality. Then it was time to leave for Spean Bridge Hotel, my rendezvous with Kai and Jim. We spent the night there, as I had arranged to stalk Killiechonate next day with two stalkers. Killiechonate was a big forest, and ran up to the summit of Ben Nevis. It had been bought by the British Aluminium Company, with two other adjacent forests, and they had harnessed all the massive water power to generate electricity, through tunnels, to their factory at Fort William.

The factor of all these forests was Sandy Kinnear, who had been a naval midshipman with me in 1940, and we often met thereafter. The two Stalkers were most welcoming and efficient. Jim and Kai took the East Beat with Stalker Sinclair and I had the West Best with Stalker Fraser. We had an excellent couple of days there, shot several stags, and were well satisfied with our visit. Then we left for the Blair Atholl Hotel with Dalnacardoch on the venue.

The three of us arrived at Sronfadrig Lodge, but there was only one Stalker, so I allotted him to Kai and said I would be Jim's Stalker. Jim and I had an excellent morning stalk, and Jim shot well – a nice eleven pointer, which I gralloched. I told Jim to walk back to Sronfadrig and get the ponyman to help to load the stag. I would take the rifle and stalk on my own, with a 7 p.m. R.V. at Sronfadrig. I climbed a high ridge and looked down on to the huge corrie Canach Choire. There were deer in it, but well below the watershed and too far out to shoot and collect. I left them alone and ascended an adjacent round mountain, which I described earlier, when I received radio directions from Rex McCulloch! I sat and rested near the summit. Far down the long glen that led to Sronfadrig, I heard a stag roar. I glassed the area in vain. The roaring continued, but the light was failing. Suddenly the stag emerged from the gloom, about 400 yards below me. A travelling stag, to be sure. He kept roaring. He was also climbing the mountain, but he was likely to be fully 300 yards when he was abreast with me.

I managed to ambush the stag at around 150 yards and shot him dead. Then I spotted Kai and Jim far below me, coming my way and obviously looking for me. They had heard the shot, and we waved to each other. By the time they arrived, I had gralloched the stag.

It was too late to consider dragging the stag, although we had three-man power, so we set off for Sronfadrig. Half way, we met Hamish the ponyman with his garron. Hamish had been a catering student at Stirling, but had failed his exams. I had engaged him as a salmon netsman two years previously, but he would be paid off at the end of August, and I got him this job as ponyman. He was a very powerful young man with a flaming red beard, and stood well over six feet. Although new to the job, he became the best and most reliable ponyman I ever met.

Hamish said he was on his way to collect my stag. It was already half dark and I tried to dissuade him. He would have none of it; he would easily manage to load the stag himself. In spite of the darkness and the very rough broken ground, Hamish was down with the stag not long after we arrived at the lodge and were enjoying a dram – or two or three!

It was back to the hotel at Blair Atholl, and we were restricted to one rifle there, so I rented two more rifles at adjacent Dalnaspidal from Colonel Hornung, so that we could all stalk independently of one another.

After this, Kai departed for Austria and Jim for USA, but I could not resist remaining for Oct. 16 and 17th at Glendoll, where I got a super right and left at heavy stags on 16th October. I had another two stags with Ian Holmes on 17th October, and then decided to call it a day for the season. It had been an excellent marathon ranging over different forests.

Chapter 7

1976–79

In 1975 Kai came over from Austria as usual, and we had a warm-up on Glendoll, then on to Dalnacardoch and Dalnaspidal, thence to Ballachulish Hotel for a stay. Here we had sub-rented Mamore Forest from 'mine host', Mr Macfarlane Barrow. Mamore is a biggish forest, and rises roughly from sea level to the highest mountain top in Britain, Ben Nevis. It was one of the huge tracts of mountainous land bought by the British Aluminium Company at the turn of the century for hydro-electric generation.

There were two Stalkers at Mamore, Sandy Masson and his son Colin. The latter had lost the lower part of one arm in a clay pigeon shooting accident, and when out stalking, his arm ended with a 'cleek' or savage looking hook, reminding one of *Treasure Island* and the pirates! Sandy and his son were both excellent Stalkers, and we much enjoyed our time there, and had some very pleasant evenings with 'mine host' after a dram – or two!

I did not find the climbing nearly as exhausting as on some other forests, possibly due to the vast funds of the Aluminium Company in driving rough tracks up to a fairly high altitude, where we could go in a 4 x 4.

Notwithstanding this, some of the downhill stalks were both steep and dangerous. One day, Kai being out with Sandy Masson, his son Colin acted as my Stalker. I was fascinated by his progress downhill over rocks and coarse heather, digging in his 'cleek' much more efficiently then I could use my arm. It was time for Kai to go home by air from Aberdeen, but I could not resist the last two days of the season at Glendoll. I got three stags.

Not long after stalking Mamore with Sandy Masson, he was chosen as Head Stalker on H.M. the Queen's magnificent forests of Balmoral, where he stayed for many years. He retired from there in 1997, and although I have never stalked on the Royal preserves, I did quite often meet Sandy helping at low-ground shoots in the district.

My game book does not mention anything exciting in 1976, except for the last day of the stalking with Ian Holmes. We climbed to the top of Craig Mellon and glassed the steep sides below us. There was a herd of Red Deer about a third of the way down, but the approach was difficult.

No cover of any use between us at the ridge summit and the deer below. We had to belly-crawl the whole way. Most carelessly I dislodged a big stone, and it raced downhill past the herd, which quickly vanished. I apologised to Ian for my negligence.

Returning to the high plateau, we saw the same herd moving out on to the Moulzie Beat of Balmoral, and I fired a shot at 200 yards and missed. Then further along the plateau we were moving towards Glendoll Hostel, which lay about 2,500 feet below in the valley of the River Whitewater, so called because of its constant small waterfalls and the speed of its current. Here we spied more deer and I missed a reasonably easy stag at 200 yards. Up to that day Ian had had a very high opinion of my stalking prowess, but I am sure that after that disastrous morning he must have changed his mind. We had lunch in gloomy silence.

Then we started along the crest of Craig Mellon towards Moulzie, spying the high tops and the valley of the River South Esk as it wound its way up to Moulzie Lodge and the end of Glenclova.

That afternoon nothing could go wrong, after a morning when nothing went right. In the space of three hours, I had slain four excellent stags with four shots. It was getting dark when I shot the last one and I wondered how the hell Ian would recover them. After all, the season was now over.

Ian made light of the situation and said he would recover all four next day, and, if I remember rightly, it was a Sunday! Sadly, it was the last time I was ever to stalk with Ian, who stood a slight wiry figure at about 5' 8" and was one of the toughest stalkers, particularly at dragging, I ever met.

Ian was under a cloud with the Estate Management that spring, and on top of that he had drink and marriage problems.

As a private guest of Lord Airlie at a grouse, pheasant and partridge shoot in Glenclova, I told him how much I had enjoyed the privilege of shooting in Glendoll for many years, but he would not accept any rent at all. I suggested I might repay it slightly by dynamiting some big rocks on Jock's Road, so that ponies could be used from Glendoll Farm right up the glen to the march with Callater/Balmoral at the north-east corner of the forest. We never stalked much beyond the shelter on Jock's Road, because we could not get the stags in or the ponies up. I should add that I was a qualified, licensed high explosives man! Lord Airlie agreed to my suggestion and that summer I arranged to meet Ian to act as my shot-fires mate and clear the obstructions. When I reached Ian's house, I found that he was not there as arranged, and was involved in some altercation with his wife etc. I was really cross, because I had made an 80-mile car journey with explosives in vain.

However, next week I tried again, collecting Sandy Mearns at Rottal and having my eldest son, aged twelve, with me to help. We had a useful half day, and I smashed all the big rocks. All that was needed was a crowbar to lever them clear of Jock's road, and they would cascade to the bottom of the valley below.

Ian never tried to shift the boulders. He had been sacked, lost his licence through drink, and lost his wife. It was a sad end to a promising career. He went off shore to an Oil Rig, and I was told he was the only man ever to work on an Oil Rig in plus fours! Later Ian became a fishing ghillie on the Tay, and we did not lose touch. We still exchange messages through mutual friends to this day (1998).

In 1977 I rented Rhidorroch, Ullapool, from Major Scobie for a week – possibly it had been advertised in the *Sporting Press*. Jim Branscome was available for three days. I thought life in the evenings might be rather dull, so I also imported female company in the form of Isobel McBain from Laurencekirk and Gina Reid from Aberdeen. I collected Jim from Aberdeen Airport, and we drove to Ullapool's Royal Hotel via Inverness. The Forest had been let for 'two stalkers' and I sublet one to a couple of Germans, who also stayed at the Royal.

On arrival at Rhidorroch, I was told that the

regular Stalker was Jackie Mackenzie, but the estate had hired another man, not really as a Stalker
but as a man who knew the ground. I therefore
allocated the experienced Stalker to the Germans.
Gina Reid decided against coming, but Isobel
McBain said she was 'game', so Jim, Isobel and I
set off with the so-called ghillie. Apart from the
fact that he had some idea of the ground, he was
quite useless. Poor man, he was also recovering
from TB and had no strength, and his eyesight for
spotting was quite hopeless. I decided I would stalk
for Jim. Isobel, who had never been stalking before, had the eyes of a lynx and was the first to
spot a nice herd near the summit of the mountain
we were climbing. We closed the herd to about
600 yards and noted a good heavy stag. I told
Isobel and the ghillie to wait there, as the ground
was pretty open and four people crawling would
be too much. Jim and I closed the range to about
130 yards and Jim made an excellent shot. The
stag ran fifty yards and dropped dead. Now we had
to get the carcase home and there was no pony.
Jim was quite exhausted and so was the ghillie,
before we even started to drag. Luckily Isobel was
a powerful girl of about 5' 10" and 12 stones, and
she and I dragged the beast down to the road
leading to the Lodge. It was sheer hard work.
Although it was mostly downhill, there were peat
runnels and flat areas where brute force was nec-

essary, but by super-human efforts we did at last reach the road, quite exhausted. Luckily the Germans had enjoyed success too, and we were all well satisfied.

Isobel had had quite enough, and for the next two days she and Gina explored the shops and sights of Ullapool while Jim and I continued stalking.

I found our beat was hopelessly disturbed by masses of people, and on investigation, found it was a film company making *The Thirty-nine steps* or some similar John Buchan novel of German spies in the Highlands. I was somewhat fed up, but what could we do except use their canteen for hot meals? Luckily, they did not trespass on the other beat, and so did not upset the Germans.

I found the sport rather indifferent. I think the Laird or one of the family was critically ill, and I did not want to make a fuss over the disturbance. Half way through my let, I had a super invitation from the new Earl of Strathmore to shoot grouse at Holwick in Yorkshire, so I packed up early, took the girls home, and put Jim on the Aberdeen/London plane before rushing off to Yorkshire.

Short as it was, I enjoyed Rhidorroch and was pleased to see the ground, which was really attractive. I was only sorry that I had failed to exploit its full potential.

The following year Kai and I jointly rented Dalnaspidal from Roger Adams, grandson of Colonel Hornung, who had sadly died at a ripe old age. Kai was married by this time, and brought his bride with him, and also his brother and sister-in-law. We stayed at Blair Atholl.

Dr Herbert Koch, Kai's brother-in-law, had never been to Scotland before, nor seen a Red Deer, so it was quite an experience for him.

I was stalking for him on one of the first days, and we were within 130 yards of a good stag. I told him to shoot when he was ready. I had already warned him that sometimes speed in firing was essential, and if he hesitated I would shoot the stag myself. Herbert made an awful mess of getting his safety catch off and the stag sensed our presence. I could not wait. Just as I fired, I heard Herbert's rifle fire also, but his bullet grazed a hind and my stag fell dead. I congratulated him on his excellent shot. In the excitement, I don't think he realised that I had fired at all. Herbert was always far too slow, but I could not blame him. After all, I had the experience of many years behind me.

After Dalnaspidal, we made our way back to Angus and beloved Glendoll! We stayed in the Jubilee Arms as usual. An excellent young, tough experienced ghillie, Raymond Hogg, was a new recruit there. One day Kai and the Stalker parted company on the Greenhill, which is a massive hill on the opposite side to Glendoll, marching with Invermark and Hunthill. I was stalking for Herbert. After spotting a good stag, I got Herbert in pretty close, and we shot it. A few minutes later Kai arrived and most indignantly told us we had shot his stag. He had seen the beast from the other side!

I don't know what Herbert thought of Scotland or of stalking, but he never returned again! I met

Stalking Boat on Loch Monar 1979. Standing – Author, Kai Head Stalker Sandy Duncan

him quite often in Austria afterwards and we remained good friends, but I think he had abandoned field sports on becoming Chief Executive of the largest furniture and carpet chain in Austria – the Leiner Group.

In 1979 I rented Pait and Monar Forests for a week from Colin Stroyan, an Edinburgh lawyer and keen stalker. I was accompanied by Kai Miedler and Surgeon Vice-Admiral Sir John Rawlins. John Rawlins was one of my friends at Wellington College in the middle thirties, and we enjoyed a great deal of field sports while we were at school there.

After a night in the Glencannich Hotel, we set off to find Pait and Monar, which were joined together as one forest. A Council road follows the course of the River Glass from the hotel towards Inverness before it becomes the River Beauly, and some miles down this road there is a long private drive leading off to the west, thence through a Spencer Nairn property, and the drive ends at the chalet at which was the Forest H.Q. Head Stalker Sandy Duncan met us there, with Second Stalker Yule. Sandy was once a Stalker at Invermark, so we had some common knowledge between us. Much of the stalking started by boating down Loch Monar in a comfortable launch, then we would land maybe a mile or so down the loch, before ascending the local mountains. This forest

"Early in August, taking it easy". Kai Miedler & Surgeon Vice Admiral Sir John Rawlins. Invercauld, Aberdeenshire

marches with Braulen to the south and Inverinate to the west. Inverinate itself runs to the Atlantic Shore.

All deer were very scarce for the first three days, and sport was pretty sparse for the two parties out. John had important engagements south and had to leave, but his replacement was Neil Findlay, who also brought his wife. Neil was factor of the Kinnaird Castle estate in Angus and I had often met him when I was shooting with Lord Southesk.

Local information was that the forest had been very heavily 'punished' by the shooting incumbents of the previous week, and that the deer had mostly vanished on to the neighbouring forests.

However, by mid-week the resident deer were returning and we had some fairly good sport. Two stalking parties were out every day.

I found it quite a tough forest. It took one a lot of walking and glassing before one got the rifle out. Stalker Yule was a good and competent stalker and guide, and very interesting to talk to about the topography and habits of the deer – very knowledgeable. One day we reached the Inverinate March, which was a long distance from where we started. We did shoot a few stags – nothing of much note. I felt it a bit unfair that the forest had been so heavily plundered the week before we arrived. I had paid £1,500 for 12 stags, and we only achieved about 50 per cent of this. Tips given were £10 per day to stalker, £4 to ghillie and £2 to ponyman – all per day. In spite of the very poor sport, the excellence of the hotel and the good company made our stay very enjoyable. Had I rented a second week, after much of the ground had been left undisturbed, I think we would have had some very good stalking. It was a picturesque forest without doubt. The last two days of the season we were back to Glendoll and the Greenhill of Clova. John Baynes was now the Stalker here, with Raymond Hogg as second man. Both knew the ground like the back of their hands, and I was particularly impressed with Raymond Hogg. I think he must have left Cortachy Estates shortly after, and if he got another job as a Stalker on some other estate, that was their good fortune.

My game book records that one day I shot a stag at 300 yards, and next day missed an easy shot at 100 yards. I noted that Kai shot very well.

In 1980 three of us decided to rent Dalnaspidal Forest for a short period, and we were to be guests in the Lodge, included in the rent with all food, for £1,200 per week from Roger Adams and his charming wife. Kai brought his wife from Austria, as did Gunther Kassner, another continental shooting chum of mine. Jim Branscome was also a guest. We were very comfortable in the Lodge and very well looked after. Sport was slightly above average, and the weather was good. Roger Adams quite often did the stalking, sharing the two rifles out with Kennedy, the Head Stalker. I did not rate Kennedy's stalking ability very high, but he was an excellent 'handyman plus' for Roger, who lived in England most of the year. Kennedy was very good at maintaining the hill transport, which included a rubber-tracked vehicle with a cabin, and several other smaller machines. If the others were fully occupied, I often stalked on my own, and remember shooting a very heavy hummel as the light was failing and Kennedy was off to help another party. I duly gralloched the hummel in the usual way, but received a rocket from Kennedy next day for failing to conform with new European regulations. All the 'bits', except for the stomach, had to be kept for inspection in plastic sachets. Apparently this was in conformity with German regulations, and Germany was the main buyer. Dalnaspidal, probably about 18,000 acres, lies to the south-west of the A9 Perth/Inverness Highway, and the march to the north-east is that road. The west beat was difficult to stalk and marched on high ground with Drumochter, which apparently had a sanctuary just over our march. It was very difficult to coax the deer over that march, and it was essential to get on to the high ground – about 3,000 feet, to stalk our beat from whichever end the wind dictated. The ground was mostly too open to consider anything else. This beat included a deep glen parallel to the Drumochter march, where the ground was steeper and it was easier to stalk. The east beat was quite different and the boundary ran along the shore of Loch Garry and rose very steeply to nearly 3,000 feet from the water. I had found that the secret lay in marching the whole length of Loch Garry from the Lodge, probably four miles, where Dalnaspidal marched with Craiganour, then along their march to ascend the massif above the loch. The ground from the

Craiganour march to the heights above was not too steep, and there was plenty of scope even to the flats to the South East of the path we took. I had shot quite a few stags on these flats. It was not too difficult because there were plenty of contiguous peat runnels to give one cover.

Once on top of the massif, it was easy to glass the long slopes down to the loch and stalking downhill on this section was quite easy, although there were a few sheer drops of 30 feet or so. But there was no dangerous moving scree. We enjoyed our stay thoroughly and the dinnertime conversations – all very good value. Kai and I got back home in time for a day trip to Glendoll on the last day of the season with Stalkers John Baynes and Raymond Hogg.

I was in the habit of letting ground for sheep to Charlie Downie, a well known flockmaster from Crathie, Braemar, who knew of my interest in stalking. Accordingly in 1980 I was invited to Glenfiddich by the Stalker Stuart Donald, son-in-law of Charlie Downie. I booked in a couple of nights at the Craigellachie Hotel, and set off to find the place. I crossed the Dee Watershed into Strathdon, then went by Lumsden and Clova to the notorious Cabrach road, always one of the first in Scotland to be snowbound and closed. It is a very lonely road, and I pulled in at a most isolated pub, the Grouse Inn, well called, as it was utterly isolated in a desert of moorland. After instructions at the inn, I found Glenfiddich Water with no difficulty, got my bearings, and spent the night at Craigellachie. I found Stuart Donald's cottage half-way between the Fiddich Water and the Grouse Inn, and was welcomed there by Stuart and his wife Aileen.

I knew from information on the grapevine that Glenfiddich, more renowned for grouse than deer, had been badly used for quite a few years, with some very poor head stalkers, who had made up numbers by shooting deer at night from Land Rovers with spotlights. The property had only quite recently been bought by Christopher Moran, an insurance entrepreneur, who, according to the national press, was the first man to be expelled from Lloyds in 200 years! Now in his early thirties, he was one of the richest men in Britain, and had already bought the adjoining Cabrach Moors, where I had shot grouse.

I very much admired the work Stuart had done and was doing. The grouse were no longer profitable through disease, and Stuart was not really interested in grouse. His great ambition was deer, and he had already made great strides by culling poor animals and avoiding shooting good heads. By the time I was stalking there, I had seldom seen so many good heads and heavy stags. However, Stuart would not let me shoot anything but rubbish, and he was quite right. I stalked Glenfiddich with him several times, and later stayed with him in his cottage.

On one occasion the rain came down in such torrents that his cottage was surrounded by water. The Fiddich runs into the Spey, but Black Water, which rises on Stuart's ground, runs into the Deveron. The feeder stream was in full flood when I left him, due to pick up Kai and his wife at Aberdeen Airport, and I never thought I would make it. However, I did, and also got an invitation for Kai to have a day there on his own.

The landowner seemed to have little interest in stalking, nor really in grouse. Maybe it was just an investment, and a retreat from the City of London!

Stuart received little encouragement over the years he was there, even though he transformed the place. The owner, copying Cliff Richard, Terry Wogan and Lady Shirley Porter, planted acres of trees on the best deer wintering ground, and ruined Stuart's dream of turning it into one of the best stocked and managed forests in Scotland. I knew he would not stay there much longer. Nor did he.

Chapter 8

1980–89

In 1980 Kai and Gunther from Austria, together with me, decided to rent Glenfernate, a fairly big forest on the Kirkmichael-Pitlochry road, a tip, really, of the Cairngorm Massif, and it marched with Fealar, one of the most isolated lodges in Scotland, and with Atholl Estates to the west and had part of the vast Ben-Y-Gloe mountain within its domain. The cost was £100 per stag. The previous owner, Sir John Heathcote Amory, MP, had recently died, and the ownership had passed to another Heathcote Amory, who ultimately became PPS to Margaret Thatcher, then resigned a Ministerial Post in John Major's Cabinet over a disagreement about policy. But I digress.

Glenfernate Lodge was not available, but we were offered the Home Farm House nearby, though we had to provide all food and services.

I recruited two Montrose lassies to staff the house for us, namely Isobel McBain and Nell Maguire.

*M.P.J's First Stag – Glenaffric 1980 with Stalker
Duncan Mclennan*

Isobel was a most capable girl, whom I previously
mentioned when I rented Rhidorroch, and she was
in charge. Isobel and Nell managed the cooking,
purchasing of food and house work most admirably
and no sporting hotel could have given us better
food and service.

On our first day out, the three of us met McGregor, the Head Stalker, and his son, who was
Second Stalker.

We split our party in two. Kai and I were to go

with the Head Stalker, and Gunter with the son,
so off we set. Kai was to use my rifle, and have
first stalk.

Just about noon, McGregor spotted a herd with
a good shootable stag, and the two of them moved
in while I stayed behind and watched.

Kai fired at a range of about 120 yards and the
stag and hinds took off at a gallop. I rejoined Kai
and McGregor. The latter was incredibly rude to
Kai, and told him if he couldn't hit a stag at that
range he would be better to stay at home. Kai was
very crestfallen and I was furious. I told McGregor
that I thought I heard the bullet strike flesh, which
he rudely pooh-poohed. We ate our sandwiches
in a dismal frosty silence. Then we plodded on,
and in under 150 yards found Kai's stag – stone
dead.

Then it was my turn to stalk, and we spied
another good herd with a stag. Kai stayed behind,
and McGregor and I got to within 400 yards when
the hinds became suspicious. I told McGregor I
would belly-crawl alone, and try to get much
closer. I had closed the range to under 210 yards,
when suddenly the deer, who had been settled and
grazing, suddenly took off. When I looked behind
I saw McGregor waving a white handkerchief. I
was more than furious, and told McGregor so very
clearly. We then trudged on for another stalk.
McGregor moved so quickly that we could barely

keep up with him. He obviously wanted to get his own back for the dressing down I had given him.

At last we spied another herd, much more easily approached than the last. We got to within 120 yards, this time on a perfect stalk, and I shot the stag dead. McGregor congratulated me on the shot. I maintained a stony silence.

Back at our Home Farm House, I rang my office and asked them to send a Telex to Jamie Illingworth, the senior partner of all shooting/fishing/stalking lets at Strutt and Parker in London.

Presumably Jamie had a pow-wow with Heathcote Amory and/or McGregor, for the atmosphere changed visibly the next day and relations became much more cordial.

I was stalking with McGregor alone one day, and we came on a big herd quite near the Lodge. We got in reasonably close to a good stag and it would not be a difficult shot. I missed it, clean. I handed the rifle to McGregor and said 'You shoot it.' McGregor fired, missed the stag and killed a hind. On a poor performance chart, we were 1–1! A draw.

We followed the herd, which was not much disturbed, and they settled on a neighbouring mini-forest, between Glenfernat and the Kirkmichael-Pitlochry road. The stag was about sixty yards the wrong side of the march. My blood was up, and I felt I might risk shooting it, but McGregor wisely refused permission. We ate our sandwich lunch and hoped the herd and stag would move back over our march. We waited a full hour, and the stag was now only 50 yards the wrong side. A shot rang out, and the stag fell dead. The stalking party on Straloch had been stalking the same stag from the other side. McGregor was quite right; I should not have been so rash as to consider risking it.

All this disturbed the locality, and McGregor decided to take the big Cherokee Jeep and drive up the glen track in the general direction of Ben-y-Gloe. Sitting in the passenger seat, I spotted a stag standing in the small river which I think is called the Ardle. I told McGregor, and we stopped on the track behind a vast peat hag and peered over. The stag was still there – motionless – standing in the river, which was no more than a foot deep in most places and about 20 yards wide. Leaving the jeep on the track, we stalked the beast and I shot it at a range of 70 yards. It fell dead in the river, which was far too shallow to float it. We waded in and pulled the beast to the bank. It seemed in perfectly good condition, but had a few stab wounds about it. McGregor told me it must have been in a big fight with another stag, had got the worst of it, and was resting and cooling down in the water before travelling on to find more hinds. In the next twenty years I never came across a similar incident.

I had several other days with old McGregor, but was never out with the son. I missed one stag at a range of 130 yards – very steep downhill shot – and I went right over the beast's shoulder. It is a very common error in shooting downhill on steep ground. However, I did get one or two good shots.

My colleagues and their wives much enjoyed our stay, and the novelty of doing our own shopping and catering. In Pitlochry, Isobel managed to buy the largest kippers I had ever seen.

I had taken some deep frozen mallard from my deep freeze, and we decided to have our roast wild duck for dinner one night. I was in my bath, thawing out after a cold wet stalk, when Isobel rushed in with the oven-ready duck on a platter. 'Smell this,' she said. I did, and the smell was appalling.

The duck was the 'pièce de résistance' for our dinner party. We had no alternative for the main course.

I told Isobel to stuff them well with herbs, cook them, and see what they were like then. Although the smell in the kitchen rekindled memories in me of Bombay Duck, the end result was terrific. No smell, and the flesh as tender as could be. There was no doubt that the duck was overripe, like some cheeses!

McGregor's attitude had completely changed by the end of the let, and he was helpful in every way, particularly in assisting with boiling the heads of the fallen and preparing them for their long journey back to Austria. We all shook hands on parting and were able to say we had much enjoyed the venture.

Then we returned to my home in Kincardineshire, and put Gunther and his wife on the London plane to wing their way back to Austria.

Kai stayed with me a few more days and we shot Glendoll on the 19th–20th October. John Baines

Success in Glendye, Kincardineshire 1982. Archie Dykes, Head Stalker with Maurice

and Second Stalker Gary Hogg were excellent, and we added three more stags to our game book.

In 1982, I took my eldest son Maurice for a day's stalking on Glendye. Archie Dykes, a beat keeper in Lord Mansfield's property of Scone Palace, had become the new Head Stalker. He was highly efficient, well organised and made a complete transformation of the deer on Glendye, but much of the credit must also go to Peter Gladstone, brother of Sir William, who actually owned all the vast properties. Maurice got a stag with some difficulty, after a very wet cold day. Peter Gladstone insisted we should call in at Fasque House on our way home – and treated us to far more Scotch than was good for me – as a driver!

In October Peter Koreska accompanied Kai from Austria and we rented two or three days at Dalnaspidal. Glendoll was always tempting me, and we spent the 19th and 20th October there, getting five stags. I noted in my book that tips to the Stalker were £15 per day, and £5 to the ghillie/ponyman.

In 1983 I went to Invermearn Forest as a guest of Alby (Hon. M.A. Bowes Lyon, younger brother of the Earl of Strathmore.) Alby gave me rough instructions on how to reach him, so with the aid of my road map I motored off. My local knowledge ran out near Aberfeldy and I took a road marked Glenlyon. I followed this to a T Junction with a bridge over the Lyon and motored on. After quite a long drive I found myself opposite Loch Tay on the Kenmore-Killin road! I retraced my route to the bridge, which I then identified as Bridge of Balgay, and taking the other road, carried on west. One of the places I passed was Cashlie Forest, and a local told me I must continue up the road to where it ended in some modern cottages. Seemingly, these cottages and the road had been built by the Hydro Board, and they had dammed up the river and tunnelled in other waters to form a fairly large loch. Apart from the fairly modern cottages, there was a larger dwelling, formerly, I think a small farm house, and here I found Alby.

He lived in the farm house and guests were based in the comfortable cottage or cottages, some of which were occupied by Hydro workers. Living quarters were most agreeable.

After a good breakfast in the farmhouse, we left to meet the Stalkers, Bob Bisset and his assistant. The estate had been bought by a Dutch/Belgian baron, and Alby was renting it.

The Head Stalker was Bob Bisset, a man with a fearsome reputation, aged in his sixties. I had heard that after an altercation with a Cabinet Minister, he had sent the gentleman home before 'half time', and I wondered how I would get on with him.

Bob Bisset was a managing man, who was pretty

brusque and businesslike. In no time he had put me in an Argo Cat, and we drove up the loch to a boathouse and straight on to a landing craft. This powered across the Loch, and as we drove off the landing craft in the Argo Cat, I felt I was part of the invasion force at Arromanches!

I discovered that Bob had been a Stalker and ghillie at Ardlair, Loch Maree, when I was stationed at Loch Ewe, and he had then had an adventurous time in the Army Commandos. We had quite a lot in common and this broke the ice to some extent. Then it was off to the hills, which were pretty high – Invermearn had five Munros on its patch.

High on the hill, Bob glassed five stags on their own, all quite settled, and we stalked them successfully, closing the range to about 120 yards. Four were grazing and the fifth was lying and dozing! 'Tak the yin lyin,' says Bob. I told him I could manage the grazing stags, but not the lying one. 'Dae as yer telt!' exclaimed Bob, and I had no option. I fired, and the stag rolled over stone dead! 'I never thought I would get that,' says I. Bob's laconic 'I kent ye wud,' was all he said. I much enjoyed stalking with Bob, and we became great friends. His early days near Poolewe and mine at Aultbea cemented our friendship and Alby very kindly asked me to stalk there during one or two of the seasons following.

At breakfast one day came word that Bob was really ill and dizzy, and quite unfit to go to the hill. Alby insisted we go and see him in his cottage, and there he was holding his head in his hands by the fire and Mrs Bisset close to weeping. I didn't think Bob was really as ill as he thought he was, and I tried to pull his leg. I told him he should go and see the doctor, who would likely prescribe a course of 'Rentokil'. This rather shocked Alby, who said he must come and see the doctor, probably in Kenmore or Aberfeldy. So I went to the hill with the very competent Under-Stalker, and we had a very pleasant day. Alby's minions provided excellent packed lunches with a thermos of straight Indian tea, laced with cloves. No sugar, no milk. It was most invigorating. I had never had it before, nor have I since.

Back at our H.Q., I asked Alby how he had got on at the doctor's, and it transpired that Bob's trouble was that he had an awful accumulation of ear wax. After he was syringed out, he was quite OK again, much to our relief.

Bob was contemptuous of all modern comforts, and refused to have television in the cottage. He was a magnificent leather worker, and his hill shoes, or brogues, were much sought after. He and his wife were great characters. He passed away shortly after he retired, before he was 70, around 1996.

In 1986, Alby rented Dunlossit from Bruno Schroeder. It was a stately home and deer forest on the island of Islay, at Port Askaig, and thither I set out in September. I was given rough instructions how to get there, and I motored by way of Forfar, Perth, Crianlarich Iverary, Lochgilphead and down Loch Fyne to Tarbert. I had never been south of Ardrishaig before, so I stopped at Tarbert, refreshed myself at the local inn, and sought instructions. Apparently the ferry ran from Loch Tarbert to Port Ellen in Islay. Putting my car on the ferry, I found some female company! This was a young mother with child, about three, who told me she was married to a Stalker on Jura, and she was getting divorced because he had abandoned her and left the island. Discovering that she had to go to Port Askaig to get the ferry over to Jura, I offered her a lift, which she gladly accepted. I had never set foot on Islay before, and Dunlossit lay at the other end of the island. The girl was not only depressed – quite naturally, but was finding the journey with the bairn and luggage almost too much, so I gave her a helping hand, and she most capably showed me the route to Port Askaig, where I put her on the Jura Ferry, then repaired to stately Dunlossit, four hundred yards from the Ferry Pier. I arrived in good time for dinner and was met by Alby and his other guests.

The mansion – or rather, castle – of Dunlossit

The Target on Dunlossit used for shooting at 2600 yards! A telephone connects a bullet proof bunker, beside the target, to the firing point

had been built in Victorian times by Bruno Schroeder's grandfather, I think, and had never been altered since then. Although luxurious, it was very outdated. It was very well staffed and the food was good, but the rent for the accommodation was naturally very expensive.

Next day we met the Head Stalker, Donald Stewart, and the Assistant Stalker, D. J. MacFee. There was a target and rifle range 100 yards from the front door, and after we had fired several rounds to the satisfaction of all, the Head Stalker and I made for the hill.

Dunlossit Forest, which fronts the Sound of Islay on the east, rises to around 2,400 at its highest. It is not particularly steep, but distances are quite considerable. I could soon observe that it was very well stocked with quality deer, all of which seemed to be very well managed. Alby rented Dunlossit for the next five years, and very kindly invited me as a guest all through that period.

My first day out was in good weather, and as we reached the higher ground, we stopped to admire the scenery. I had proudly taken my first naval command through the Sound of Islay forty-five years earlier in 1941, and little could I have imagined as a very young naval officer that I would be privileged to stalk on the island all these years later. I had an excellent week there, and found Donald Stewart one of the nicest men on the hill I had ever met. We seemed to have a very good understanding of one another, and I shot several stags.

Then I had to scuttle back to Kincardineshire, where I was to pick up Kai for more local stalking. Back at Glendoll one day, a young man named Bill Mearns was my Stalker, and I think I allocated Head Stalker John Baynes and the best beat to Kai on Craig Mellon.

Bill and I travelled up Jock's Road nearly to the watershed and the waterfall, which I had named the Mare's Tail. It was a magnificent waterfall when in flood, quickly falling over 1,000 feet, all white water, into the river aptly called the White-water, which flowed into the South Esk near Glendoll Lodge. We left Jock's Road at a very rough shelter, which had been built by hill walkers to commemorate the tragic death of an entire group of hill walkers who had set out to hike from Braemar to Glendoll. It was on New Year's Day, 1951, if I remember correctly.

Bill and I were to stalk the precipitous Craig Rennet, on the side of the Whitewater opposite to Craig Mellon. Once the shelter had been reached, the ground became flatter, and a gradual slope ran up to the summit. This was close to the march with Tulchan and Glenisla. So there we were at around 2,500 feet, with a superb view of Glendoll.

The side of Craig Rennet is very steep and dangerous, and access to the valley below should only be taken by the very experienced. There are only certain routes – maybe as few as five along the valley – that it is safe to take. There were several herds below us, and a good stiff wind from the west funnelling down the valley – suitable for a stalk of one herd that Bill had spotted.

With great difficulty we descended about 800

feet, where we were at the same altitude as the beasts. Bill got me in very well, with much crawling, and I shot my stag. It was the only time I met and stalked with Bill, but I thought he was a lad of great promise.

I last heard of him as a full-time Stalker on Mar Lodge, one of the most famous forests in Scotland, so my assessment of him cannot have been far wrong.

The next year, back at Dunlossit, I remember having a good day with Second Stalker D.J. Macphee, always known as D.J. He was a very competent man, and I had a good stalk and shot a fine stag without difficulty. My second stalk was not so successful, and I wounded a beast which I should have killed outright, but after a long hard chase we caught up with it, and this time I made sure of it.

Alby and I decided we would have a day off next day, and explore the neighbouring island of Jura. The twin 'Paps of Jura' showed up beautifully in the sunlight. The Sound is under a mile wide, and the ferry runs about every hour. I drove on to the island and round the south top, then up the coast with great views on to the mainland of Argyll. A third of the way up the coast, we came to the Jura Hotel and the Distillery. I couldn't resist tasting the famous Jura whisky, and at the same time explored the hotel – the only one on the island. Then we drove north up the coast to where the tarmac and Council road ended. We glassed some very fine herds between the road and the sea – the road was often two miles from the shore.

Arriving at the end of the road, we tried a track which led to the north, but it was quite unsuitable for an ordinary car so we had to turn back. I had always wanted to stalk on Jura, and suggested we should call on the local laird, who owned Ardlussa Forest. His grandfather was a distinguished Naval Captain in Aberdeen and a friend of my parents, who had given me a lot of help when he was Captain of Coastguards for East Scotland. I also knew his grandmother, who had a property near Stonehaven, so all this helped as an introduction. After a chat in the house, we found out that the stalking at Ardlussa could be rented, but was heavily booked by Danes every year. The details were useful, and I determined to stalk it another year, as did Alby. Then it was back to Dunlossit and Ardtalla, where Alby had kindly arranged for me to stalk next day.

Ardtalla was a new forest to me, and I had to find it. Although much of it marched with Dunlossit, it required a motor drive of over forty miles to get there, and I had to run right back to Port Ellen and take a side road, which ran up the Sound of Islay, past two very famous distilleries, one being

Leophraig. The road ended in a cul-de-sac where estate roads led off to the Head Stalker's House with kennels, bothy etc., and so to Ardtalla House.

Ardtalla had been bought since the Second World War by Sir John McTaggart, Bart., who had made his money in the Far East. He had divorced his wife, Lady Rosie McTaggart, whose story is perhaps worth telling here. On her divorce, Lady Rosie set up in Knockie Lodge, Inverness-shire, with her own forest. She employed a Head Stalker, an ex-Commando Sergeant, and the couple became very close to one another. Then a third man appeared who displaced the Stalker-ex-Sergeant, and in a fit of jealousy he tried to murder Lady Rosie with rifle fire. He failed, was duly arrested, and got a long term of imprisonment. The scandal was very widely reported in the Scottish Press, and Lady Rosie sold up and moved to other sporting quarters in the Republic of Ireland. Sir John had died about the time I first visited Ardtalla, and his son had succeeded. Apparently Lady Rosie stayed there quite often, but sadly I failed to meet her. She must have been quite a character.

I digress. I arrived at the Kennels and met the Head Stalker. This was Gillian, head of a staff of four, and the only female Head Stalker I ever met and she was certainly one of the most competent. Probably aged in her thirties, she had been promoted from Assistant Stalker. She was of

Scottish–Swiss extraction, about 5' 9", slim, and of great muscular strength. She was not one to stand any nonsense, and was a superb stalker, pony handler, mechanic with the Argocar and did first-class work supervising the skinning and cutting up of carcases. She was also a first-class keeper with rearing pheasants and took charge of shooting parties after woodcock, for which the area was well known.

After I had satisfied Gillian with my prowess at the target, we moved off on to the forest. It was very foggy, and to begin with, we saw some deer, but because of the dense fog, never had the chance of a shot.

However, late in the afternoon the fog cleared to some extent. We had a nice stalk and I shot a stag. I thanked Gillian for an excellent day, and hoped I would be back another season.

I left Dunlossit with Alby and other guests still there, and returned to Kincardineshire for some business commitments. However, before the season ended, Kai arrived from Austria with Michel Stegner, and we were able to stalk out on Glendoll, and my eldest son Maurice joined us.

Michel Stegner was not interested in stalking, but very happy when hill walking in the foothills, so Maurice and I went with the Assistant Stalker while Kai went with John Baynes. Kai's health was not good at the time, and he elected to go with Michel the second day and give stalking a miss. So I allocated Maurice to the Head Stalker for Craig Mellon, and said I would potter about Craig Rennet with the Assistant Stalker. Unfortunately I have forgotten his name, but by trade he was in the building industry in Kirriemuir, and only assisted at Glendoll as a hobby. Notwithstanding that, he knew the ground, was very fit, and fully competent.

Walking up Jock's Road, we saw two herds grazing the very steep slopes of Craig Rennet, but they were going higher and higher. The right way to stalk Craig Rennet, as I have said before, was to go right up to the Shelter and climb to the summit, thereby being above all beasts below on the steep sides. However, we were sure that by the time we had accomplished all this – probably three hours – the beasts would have grazed to the top and over the march into Tulchan or Glenisla. The summit was always pretty wind-swept.

So the stalker and I agreed on an almost impossible task: to cross the Whitewater and only climb as high as we needed to get the same height as the deer, traversing the mountain at the same level. We might make contact before they got over the top.

It was a most exhausting business, dangerous and difficult. As soon as we were level with the deer, they had grazed higher, and we had to pick our way among the precipitous rocks and loose scree. The chase went on for at least two hours, and as soon as we thought we were on the same level, the beasts had climbed higher. So it went on. Eventually the deer beat us and went over the top and out of sight. We rested on that summit of the Craig Rennet Ridge quite exhausted. The young Stalker congratulated me on making it, and I shall never forget his remark: 'I hope I can do that at your age.' I think this effort triggered my impending heart trouble; I was then 67.

Once we were on the summit ridge, a blizzard struck. It was not nearly as bad as that in which Ian Holmes and I nearly lost our lives, but it was quite intense. We trudged along the ridge, taking shelter as necessary, until we came to the Kilbo Path, which takes one out of the bottom of Glenprosen to Glendoll and Glenclova. There I spied a good herd of deer on the very bare face of Driesh opposite us.

We were far too conspicuous on this bare ground to move in, but after around two hours, taking advantage of the thick snow showers, we got to within 300 yards of them. The light was failing and the snow showers were unsettling the deer. It was very difficult to get close. Each time we moved, the deer moved, and they were going higher. At last they spotted something very suspicious and moved to the ridge above us. The stag was a very poor target. It was difficult in that light to determine which was a stag and which was a hind. Antlers did not show against the background but one beast seemed much more bulky than the others, and at this I fired, at a range of about 200 yards.

The beast fell, then cascaded down the steep face. Regretfully, it was a heavy hind – not the stag at all, and in any case the carcase was badly damaged in the fall.

The day was a great disappointment to both of us, and was no reflection on the Stalker. Luckily, Maurice had better luck and got his stag.

Not long after this, I had to seek medical help for my heart condition. Sadly it was the last time I was fit enough to stalk Glendoll.

In 1987 I was back at Dunlossit. Another guest was Alastair Turnbull, the factor of the Strathmore Properties and Grouse Moors in North Yorkshire, who had shot his first stag with me at Hunthill on the day the late Earl of Strathmore was buried. Alby resolved to allocate Donald Stewart to me, and decided that he would accompany us and bring his rifle in case there was a chance of a second stalk.

Dunlossit is not nearly so steep as Glendoll or Dalnacardoch but it is fortunate in having lots of hummocks behind which both deer and stalker can hide.

Walking along one of the smallish glens there, Donald spied a herd, and soon we were stalking them. Without great difficulty we got behind a hillock within 140 yards of the herd, which was dominated by a heavy stag with a good head, but I couldn't make out the points. Donald told me to shoot when I was ready and the beast was broadside on. I fired and the beast fell, and, with a few kicks in the air, lay dead. To my astonishment, I found it was a superb 13 pointer

The Deer Sledge at Ardtalla, Isle of Islay. Head Stalker Gillian on left, with Rifle. 1993

Imperial, in perfect condition. Whether Alby and Donald recognised beforehand what my target was, they never let on.

After gralloching the stag, it was Alby's turn for a stalk, and we ascended the high ground. I got very out of wind near the summit, and had to take quite a few whiffs of my mini-aerosol, which gave me a second wind. Near the summit and ridge of this range of hills, Donald spied another herd. I stayed behind with a grandstand view of operations.

Donald got Alby in to about 130 yards, and Alby made a perfect shot. Thus ended a most pleasant day on the hill.

A most entertaining guest at Dunlossit was Piffa Schroeder, who had been married to Bruno, the owner; I think that at the break-up settlement, she had gained some interest in Dunlossit and the stalking. She was a most competent shot and a very knowledgeable stalker. I believe she was responsible for a huge rifle target on the forest. It was about 20 feet by 20 feet, white, with a black bull in the centre, and competitions were held in the non-stalking season, to fire at the target from ranges of up to 1,800 yards! Piffa was also a *Shooting Sports* writer of some renown.

During this same week I was out with Donald one foggy day, and we stopped to eat our lunch, staring at this target about 180 yards away. Although I never heard or saw anything approaching, I suddenly observed a large single stag disappear behind the target. We were both sitting in Donald's 4 x 4 and I alerted him. While the stag was obscured by the target, Donald told me to get out, load the rifle, and shoot when the stag emerged. It was quite an easy shot, in spite of the drifting fog, and I killed it without trouble. It was a novel and eerie experience.

Next year, in 1988, Nicole Arnaud from Monte Carlo was staying with me at Ecclesgreig and we were both invited by Alby to go to Islay.

After a good breakfast at 'The Little Chef' in Crianlarich, we caught the ferry with the car at West Loch Tarbert, then motored to Dunlossit, about 25 miles from Port Ellen, where the ferry had landed us.

Bruno Schroeder was doing a huge modernisation effort to his 'mansion', and we all stayed in the pub at Port Askaig. Really it was more comfortable than the massive, old-fashioned Dunlossit. One day was booked for me at Ardtalla, and Gillian had provided a Clydesdale-cross Garron to transport me up the steepest parts. Nicole, who was about fifty and of fairly slight build, had a magnificent physique. She brought up the rear of our cavalcade without any show of fatigue.

We did several stalks at herds just off the plateau, all unsuccessful, and our last chance came when we spotted a herd below the ridge on the west side. The weather had changed. The wind howled, bringing showers of sleet and watery snow.

Nicole stayed well behind, and the ponyman and horse were far back. Gillian and I got within a hundred yards of a stag, and I waited for a broadside shot. I discussed the situation with Gillian alongside, thinking the wind would drown any noise I made. I was wrong. The deer heard me, were suspicious, and started to move out. The stag stopped at 150 yards, broadside on, and roared defiantly. I took my chance and fired. The stag didn't seem to flinch, and I never heard any telltale 'thwack' of a bullet hitting flesh. I thought I had missed. All this had me quite exhausted, and my state was not helped by the mortification of missing the beast.

Nicole joined us on the bare snow-wracked face, and the very tough Gillian said she would follow up the beast for a short way. We all saw the herd of hinds disappear in the far distance, but there was no sign of the stag.

Gillian disappeared from sight about 400 yards downhill of us, behind a peat hillock, then reappeared waving a white handkerchief. She had found the stag, dead from a classic heart shot. We were all delighted, and celebrated with a very good dram to warm us up.

The ponyman brought up the horse, towing a

sort of sledge, and the stag was dragged about five miles, luckily nearly all downhill, to the Land Rover. Much of the time, the carcase was dragged with the skin scraping the earth, and I thought it would be badly damaged, but it was not. The ground was very wet and boggy, and this seemed to save the carcase from being trashed. I shot another two stags with Donald James before leaving to catch the afternoon ferry with Nicole.

After docking, we motored to Oban to find one of the hotels with which Oban abounds. Every hotel was fully booked, and this was late September. We motored on to Tyndrum, where there was a profusion of hotels. These offered B. & B. in the spring for £15 per person. Every one was fully booked, but the helpful proprietor of one hotel told us to try the B. & B. near Crianlarich. We managed to book the last room – a double! Nicole was not in the least put out by this, though it was far from 'en suite', and after a really good old-fashioned country breakfast, we drove back to Kincardineshire.

.

Chapter 9

1989 – The last years

The year 1990 found me back at Dunlossit where the lodge had now been refurbished. Kai and his wife accompanied me. The stalking charges and the cost of accommodation in Dunlossit were astronomic, and, we thought, a very unfair burden on Alby, so we decided to pay back our full share of both.

Alby had other guests besides us, including two German barons, and a prince or duke, who, I understood, was a near claimant to the Hapsburg throne. Donald was about to retire, and like me, feeling his age. We decided to stalk the low ground on the fringe of conifer plantations, and avoid climbing steep hills. In torrential rain, we spotted a herd with a good stag on the flat about half a mile away and started to stalk them. At about 600 yards, we were knee-crawling when they became suspicious. Donald said we would have to belly-crawl. There was no alternative.

Belly-crawling for 450 yards is a most exhausting exercise. The ground was sodden and the rain never stopped. The crawl took us about 2½ hours, stopping now and again as the herds sniffed the air and looked about them. At last we were prone and the stag grazing at 200 yards range. We were soaked and frozen! My hands were so cold I doubt if I could have pulled the trigger. I rubbed them together till some warmth returned. The stag started walking towards us, gathering in his hinds, and at 110 yards Donald told me to fire when I was ready. I made a good job of this, and the stag fell dead. Knowing that this was likely to be our last stalk together, Donald and I really celebrated. Luckily we were not breathalysed on our journey back to Dunlossit.

Alby was hard pressed to find stalking beasts for us all, and it was arranged that I would have a day on Jura at Ardlussa. I got up early, caught the Jura Ferry, and motored to Ardlussa, the journey taking me two to two-and-a-half hours. Here I was introduced to Peter Campbell, the Head Stalker. I had heard that Peter was an independent type of man, gruff and not too friendly to casual stalking guests. I found him quite the opposite, most friendly and knowledgeable, and only too keen to place his vast local knowledge at my disposal.

Ardlussa appeared to run on the top third, the north, of the island. It was not nearly so precipitous as the south, where the Paps are. It was delightful stalking country for someone with physical defects like me at this stage, very reminiscent of picturesque Flowerdale.

The stalking was very heavily booked by rich Danes, who stayed in the Jura Hotel, and I was only allowed to shoot one stag out of the annual allocation – about 40 I believe.

The Forest seemed very well stocked. Having ascended the local high ground, we glassed a big expanse between this and the Sound, far beyond. There were several herds with excellent stags. Peter decided on our quarry, and off we set. The stalks were most interesting and not too difficult. There were lots of big rocks and moss studded hillocks. At 120 yards, the whole herd was in comfortable range, and I shot the stag without difficulty. The time was not even 1 p.m., and we had our lunch.

I asked Peter if I could see more of the ground, and maybe do some stalks without shooting. He was an excellent Stalker, even if the ground was quite easy, and I could easily have shot another three stags.

Returning to the Home Farm House, where the Laird was based, we came to a Lochan, where there was a complete field of dense rhododendrons, about 20 acres in extent. Peter told me that they spread like weeds, and were a great inconvenience.

A former laird had planted a few as winter shelter for the deer, and they had proliferated out of all proportion and were a total waste of space. I had seen the same problem at Glamis Castle after the Second World War, when labour and machinery and cash had been scarce, but eventually the Laird got down to the obstacle with a bulldozer, and the problem was completely solved. I parted the best of friends with Peter, and returned to Dunlossit.

I had one or more days at Ardtalla with a new Second Stalker. This was Calum Sharpe of Glenisla, where his father was Head Stalker. He was a competent young man of about 23, and within a few years was to take over as Head Stalker from Gillian, who went to get married.

I was successful with Calum, who had got to know the ground quickly, and I enjoyed my days and sport out with him. Then it was to be a day with my old friend Gillian. Gillian was extremely good to me, and saved me all unnecessary exhaustion. Either an Argocat or a Weasel took much out of the hard grind. Sadly I think the Clydesdale Garron had died or been pensioned off.

We had a hard day trying to get to grips with several herds, but we were always defeated. The noise of the vehicles may not have helped. At last, about four p.m., we sighted a herd with several stags. We were close to two, at around 100 yards, and I told Gillian I was fairly sure of downing one.

'No, not those,' says she, 'take the far stag.' This was at least 180–200 yards, in a poor light, and I knew my rifle needed re-zeroing. It was shooting to the left. I remonstrated, but to no avail. The beast was not broadside, but half so, grazing away and slowly increasing the range. It was now or never. I put the cross wires on the beast's left haunch, in the hope that the bullet would strike the stag much nearer the shoulder, and then I fired. The stag collapsed. 'You've haunched it,' says Gillian. I was over the moon that I had got it! In great exaltation I slapped her bum alongside me, and said: 'Never mind, I got it'. Gillian quickly replied 'You're an old rascal.' I can never forget this rejoinder of hers!

I never stalked with Gillian again and within two years she had left to get married. She was just about the best Head Stalker I ever met in the West. In charge of four or five, she never faltered, and had a perfect knowledge and understanding of all the requirements of an absentee Laird and all the problems that can arise in such a remote spot as Ardtalla. I was sure she would be greatly missed.

Alby kindly asked me back in 1991, also Kai and his wife Thérèse, and Alastair Turnbull and his wife were staying there too. Alby had also invited Peter Fawcet, record-breaking Head Keeper of Holwich Moor in North Yorkshire. Peter had brought Holwich, and to some extent Wemmergil, out of the doldrums by exterminating the foxes, and had made it one of the premier grouse moors of the U.K. He was much fêted by the rich and famous, Joe Nickeson and Tom Cowie, to name but two, and it was sad when he left to get an astronomic wage from oil multi-millionaire, Sheik Makhtoum, who had bought Bollihope from my second cousins, the Pease brothers of Darlington and Barnard Castle.

As usual, it was difficult to get enough beats to keep everyone entertained, but on this occasion I was to go with Donald James, and Alastair Turnbull would accompany me as a non-shooting guest.

Just prior to setting off, Alby and I had a friendly chat about stalkers' tips. I thought £30 was a fair average; Alby thought £40. The matter was not decided.

Donald James was now the Head Stalker, and off we set. The weather was sunny, with not much of a breeze. At length, panting and rather exhausted, I made the highest ground and Donald James spotted a herd with a good stag. With little difficulty, we closed the range to 80 yards.

The stag was a beautiful Royal. Rightly, D.J. told me to leave it, and I stared into its face at under 80 yards. It was most tantalising, and the stag seemed totally settled. It was most interesting to

observe it and the rest of the herd – quite unsus-
pecting – for nearly an hour. Then we decided to
have our lunch and the stag saw us and took off.

Shortly afterwards, D.J. spotted a big herd with
a large stag on top of a cliff, just above the Sound
of Islay. It was not an easy stalk; the ground was
very open. Anyway, we got to within 180 yards,
but the light was no longer too good. I fired and
missed and was much mortified. All the deer
moved off, but they had not seen us, and did not
appear all that scared.

We had to regain much of the height we had
lost during the stalk, and we found that same herd
again near the bottom of a glen, but grazing uphill
fairly fast. With difficulty, we got to the bottom
of the glen unobserved, but the deer had grazed
well up the slope of the glen, and were at least
200 yards away. Then they got suspicious.

I fired and missed. In exasperated frustration, I
reloaded and fired again. The range was nearly
200 yards. I hit the stag alright, but too far back,
and although very hard hit, it never fell, and
staggered on after the hinds. It kept stopping and
was not far from being mortally wounded. A third
shot finished its life. It was a magnificent 14
pointer Imperial with a heavy body, and the head
was later adjudged to be the best head shot in
Scotland that year.

All this had taken us miles and miles from our

The Authors second imperial – 13 Pointer Dunlossit.
Stalker Donald Stewart on left

transport. It was dusk by now, and while D.J. did the gralloch, Alastair and I started the long walk to the vehicles. By the way we went, it was over six miles, stumbling over rough ground and crossing lots of rushing burns. I was taking frequent inhalations from my 'puffer', and by the time we arrived at the vehicles, I really was 'all in'. However, after a mighty dram of Bruchladdich I felt a lot better, and D.J. drove us home.

2.10.91 Dunlossit, Islay

I do not know if D.J. had recognised the stag, but it had really been selected for a German/Austrian princeling. I now think that I, a rather insignificant person without a title, should never even have fired at it. Whether I should or shouldn't was never cleared up. Nor could I fathom

Alby's feelings on the matter. He told me I had shot a magnificent beast, probably the very best on Dunlossit. He asked me 'What tip are you giving D.J.?' My thoughts were still working it out when Alby said 'One hundred pounds, and no argument'. So that was that.

D.J. was very good, sending the head to a lady taxidermist in practice near Gatwick, and I visited her at work. She made a splendid job for £1,000 and the head adorns the wall of my library with no other competition.

This marathon effort of the Great Imperial at Dunlossit really marked the end of my serious stalking life. It really was a wonderful finish to so many years of stalking, gaining me the finest head I ever shot. In 1992 I rested on my laurels, and took a gun in a syndicate for driven grouse at Coignafearn in Inverness-shire. This was not only a very good grouse moor, but also an excellent deer forest.

However, an advertiser in the *Dundee Courier* in the summer of 1993 rekindled the dying embers of my stalking years. It offered day lets on Hunthill and Invermark, both of which I knew were very well stocked, and where there was no shortage of well trained staff and recovery aids.

So my son Maurice and I opted for a day at Hunthill, and took a place also for my old shooting friend, David Gillanders of Aberdeen. Maurice and I shared a rifle but the stags were all far out in high, difficult terrain, and I decided to let Maurice stalk alone with David Wilson, who had been an Assistant Stalker years before when Alastair Turnbull shot his first stag there. I was able to glass the whole operation, which required a lot of stamina for crawling. The approach led up a fairly open burn to near the summit of the ridge where the deer were grazing, albeit a bit unsettled.

Maurice and David made an excellent stalk, and Maurice made a good shot at 160 yards. We were well pleased with our day, which cost £235 per stag with a £30 tip to the stalker. David Gillanders also had a successful day, and was so bitten by the sport that he immediately booked several more days on his own, plus several more at the hinds!

I then took a day at Invermark, again with Maurice and in pouring rain. The Head Stalker thought that with the mist and heavy rain we should put it off, but I decided we would have a cup of tea and wait a bit. We had driven 40 miles for this.

The rain eased a bit, and we fired at a target near the Lodge, then decided to move out into the Deer Forest proper. We stopped on a high ridge – I think near the march with Glenmuick, left the Land Rover there, and proceeded on foot. My Stalker was Ron Hepburn, a man probably in his early thirties, and very experienced and keen.

We walked in the general direction of the Airlie Forests of Greenhill of Glenclova and Glenmoy, and the mist cleared to quite good visibility. Deer were remarkably scarce in this area, which surprised me, but it was near the end of the stag season, and I think the ground had been heavily stalked.

We sighted a good herd of deer, with one or two good stags, about three-quarters of a mile away – pretty unsettled but coming in our direction. We tried to cut them off, but they kept trotting on at a good pace at around 300 yards – very hard to make out in peat runnels. I had the rifle, and I knew it was the only chance I had that day.

A good stag came into view, trotting quite smartly and not stopping. It was now or never. I put the cross wires ahead of the beast, and as it came into view in the outer circle of the sight, I fired. The stag collapsed stone dead. I was more than pleased.

The stag was loaded and then Ron asked me if I would manage the return journey to the Land Rover, which was several miles away, across a valley, up a ridge and beyond. My heart trouble was pretty acute by then, and I really had my doubts whether I could make it. However, a New Zealand student/ponyman came to the rescue. He made excellent rope stirrups on a spare garron, and I rode the whole way back with no great effort.

Glenmoy, Angus. Head Stalker Stuart Donald with Assistant –
Ormiston, grandson of the Markey Tycoon. 1990

We were all delighted with our day. As we motored
along the track, past the stables of Lee, there were
masses of deer of all sexes and sizes. They were
pouring in from the great outback to the lush grass
in the plain at the top of Loch Lee, and near the
remote stalker's cottage at Inchgrundle. It was dusk
by this time. There were a lot of easy shots although the light was well faded, but we were quite
satisfied with our well-earned trophy, and were
not tempted to shoot any more.

In the years up to 1996, I had the odd day out with Stuart Donald at Glenmoy, but on the whole was not successful. Glenmoy is really a grouse moor, and although Stuart has managed as many as 60 stags and over 100 hinds in a season, one has to be very fit and do a lot of crawling, for which I was no longer able.

I enjoyed my days out with Stuart – he was very knowledgeable and good with ponies and vehicles. I had shot quite a few hinds with him in the past, including one stalk when I shot two hinds with one barrel!

It was nice to talk over the times when I had been fit for the hill, but now, in the middle seventies, I could not stand the pace. I decided that in future I would just go out and watch, and in the past year or so I have enjoyed doing just that.

It is nice to look back on all those years since I shot my first stag at the age of 20. Nearly all stalking then was by private invitation. By 1950 it was becoming commercialised. To shoot a stag cost an average of £5. In 1998 the price is nearer £450.

By the millennium, with so many hikers and ramblers on the hills, stalking may be virtually finished. Glendoll is the classic example. There are now more ramblers then deer. The magnificent stalking on Balmoral Estates has now been en-

larged by the purchase of Glendoll from Lord Airlie, but whether it will be a bonus or a hardship
has yet to be seen.

Appendix I

Alphabetical List of Deer Forests/Grouse Moors stalked by Author.

NAME   LOCATION

A.

Achnacarry	Fort William, Inverness-shire
Alladale	Bonar Bridge, Sutherland
Alvie	Aviemore, Inverness-shire
Ardlussa	Isle of Jura, Argyll
Ardochy	Invergarry, Inverness-shire
Ardtalla	Port Ellen, Isle of Islay, Argyll

B.

Ballindalloch Castle	Ballindalloch, Banffshire
Ben More	Assynt, Sutherland
Ben Wyvis	Garve, Ross-shire

C.

Cawdor Castle	Cawdor, Morayshire
Ceannaroc	Glenmoriston, Inverness-shire
Coignafearn	Tomatin, Inverness-shire
Culachy	Fort Augustus, Inverness-shire

D.

Dalnacardoch	Calvine, Perthshire
Dalnaspidal	Calvine, Perthshire
Dalmunzie	Blairgrowrie, Perthshire
Dunmaglass	Strathnairn, Morayshire

F.

Fairburn	Muir of Ord, Ross-shire
Flowerdale	Gairloch, Ross-shire
Forest Lodge	Nethy Bridge, Inverness-shire

G.

Gaick, Kincraig	Inverness-shire
Glen Affric	Cannich, Inverness-shire
Glencannich	Cannich, Inverness-shire
Glendoll	Kirriemuir, Angus
Glendye	Banchory, Kincardineshire
Glengarry	Invergarry, Inverness-shire
Glenisla	Blairgowrie, Perthshire
Glenmoy	Kirriemuir, Angus
Glenogil	Brechin, Angus
Greenhill of Clova	Kirriemuir, Angus

H.
Hunthill   Edzell, Angus

I.
Inverlael   Ullapool, Wester Ross
Invermark   Edzell, Angus
Invermearn   Killin, Perthshire

K.
Killiechonate   Spean Bridge, Inverness-shire
Kintradwell   Brora, Sutherland

M.
Mamore   Ballachulish, Inverness-shire

P.
Pait & Monar   Beauly, Inverness-shire

R.
Rhidorroch   Ullapool, Ross-shire
Rhidorroch   Glenshee, Perthshire
Rottal   Kirriemuir, Angus

T.
Tillypronie   Aboyne, Aberdeenshire
Tor Castle   Fort William, Inverness-shire

Index

Index